# ENDORSEMENTS

"I am so thankful for Debby Sibert – for her writing, for her teaching, and for her life! She is the real deal. She loves God's Word, and she loves helping people experience abundant life according to God's good design. You will be blessed, encouraged, challenged, and ultimately changed by God's grace through her."

*David Platt, New York Times Best Selling Author*
*Lead Pastor, McLean Bible Church*

"Debby Sibert has written about someone she knows very well—Jesus Christ. In her brief, elegant account, she explains why she wants you to know him too—your future is riding on it and time is urgent. In her winsome style she pulls no punches about what's at stake – not only your destiny in Heaven or Hell but also your identity and purpose in life now.

Debby's written in a way that followers of Christ will find much to excite and deepen their faith and for those being drawn to Christ will sense Christ's heart for the lost, lonely and broken. You'll learn much about God, yourself, your neighbors and why the gospel is such a grand and glorious life-giving proclamation in this bad news world.

*Where Will You Spend Eternity? Not Sure? There's Still Time* offers a challenging and rewarding journey into the only hope and only satisfaction anyone can have—knowing, pursuing and delighting in God. Read it, share it, and live in light of the truth and grace it teaches."

*Dave Brown. Pastor, Washington Area Coalition of Men's*
*Ministries (WACMM)*

I love how this book starts off with a Wedding Singer and then quickly gets to the point: Where will you spend eternity? The author has a clear concern for the lost and the well-being of others.

She offers a reliable definition of what it means to be a Christian, as well as an explanation of what Sin really is. Important concepts are addressed like: "the desires of our heart vs. God" and "just being good vs. godly humility and submission" and "spiritual fruit."

Did you know that God has no grandchildren? Read on to learn why. Did you know that death itself can be conquered? Are there unforgivable elements of your own past? This book is an informative and comforting assurance that Jesus loves you. And that Jesus proves to be the only way to eternal life and heaven. You can have a new, better identity and it comes with unlimited eternal security. What are the Next Steps? This book provides reliable answers and guidance.

*Joe Kelty. Former Men's Pastor at McLean Bible Church*
*Director of Chaplain Support at Good News Jail & Prison Ministry*

"Debby's book, *Where Will You Spend Eternity,* answers life's most important question. She describes in a readable way how everyone can actually know the answer to their future. I commend to you not only her book, but also Debby as a genuine, kind, lay person committed to communicating to the world what she herself has experienced."

*Dale Sutherland, USA President, International Caring Ministries*
*(ICM)*

Ponder these questions with me:

- Do you sometimes wish you were better equipped to direct conversations with pre-believers about spiritual things?

- How solid are you in the "basics of the faith". Do you have a "know so" assurance of your salvation and eternal life, or is there still a lingering residue of "hope so" assurance?

- Have you been in a conversation with a believer who begins talking about spiritual things with a "personal bent" that seems to be a bit off-center, and you're not quite sure what's "off" about their perspective?

My friend and ministry colleague Debby Sibert has a gifted ability to make complex spiritual truths simple and touchable. Her writing style is purposely somewhat casual as if we are sitting down together in a warm and comfortable setting and talking about spiritual things as friends. Nothing preachy, condescending, or guilt-inducing, but good honest theological truth presented in easy-to-understand language.

I highly recommend that you peruse this easy read entitled "Where Will You Spend Eternity". It is personally encouraging in my spiritual journey and I found myself often thinking "I like how Debby puts that". In this book, you'll sense Debby's genuine compassion for people wherever they are in their spiritual journey, and her desire to be used by God to be an ambassador for the Good News (Gospel) of Jesus Christ that is available to all. You will be blessed.

*David Sheets, Ministry Leader, Coach,*
*Counselor, Speaker, and Worship Leader*

# WHERE WILL YOU

# SPEND ETERNITY?

## NOT SURE?

## THERE'S STILL TIME

# WHERE WILL YOU
# SPEND ETERNITY?

## NOT SURE?

## THERE'S STILL TIME

*DEBBY SIBERT*

## A NOTE FROM THE AUTHOR:

*It is my heart's desire that everyone would have an opportunity to meet Jesus – to experience Him intimately, to have their hearts transformed by His love and grace, and to learn the peace, joy, and victory that comes from a "sold-out" life of surrender and obedience. Do you know Him?*

*It is my passion to help people discover their life's purpose while empowering them to unlock their God-given potential.*

# ACKNOWLEDGMENTS

To my wonderful husband, who has sacrificed many days and nights of solitude while I worked tirelessly on this manuscript. Thank you also for your prayers, for proofreading, editing, and providing your valuable feedback along the way. God has used you mightily to help me become the wife, mother, friend, and Christ-follower I am today. You inspire me with your life of honesty, integrity, and servant leadership, as well as your love and devotion. This just scratches the surface of your many qualities I hope have rubbed off on me over these forty years of sharing life together. You are my rock. Thank you for believing in me and supporting me to fulfill God's purpose in finally getting this book out of my head and heart and into print.

I also thank my many friends—you know who you are, who have cheered me on and given me your feedback along the way. Your input, friendship, and love have been priceless, and I appreciate it so much! Many thanks also to my very accomplished and helpful editor, Pam Lagomarsino (AbovethePages.com).

To my pastor of almost thirty years, Lon Solomon, who unknowingly consistently mentored me from the pulpit, inspiring me to speak the truth about the gospel boldly, I thank you. My current pastor, David Platt, I thank you for the continuing challenge to deepen my faith and live it out daily with a mission mindset. Both of you have contributed greatly to my understanding of the importance of total surrender and obedience.

Most of all, I thank God for giving me a burden for lost souls and a desire to share the wonderful news of the gospel and to give hope through this medium. Lord, I thank You for saving my life through the sacrificial death of your Son, giving me eternal life in heaven with You. I thank You that the same is possible for every person reading this book. Thank You for pursuing the heart of the person reading this right now. I pray that someday You will introduce us in heaven. Amen!

# TABLE OF CONTENTS

# INTRODUCTION

Have you made your reservation yet for heaven? Do you know if your name is written in the Lamb's Book of Life? Not sure? Let me share a story I found on Randy Alcorn's blog.

Ruthanna Metzgar, a professional singer, tells a story that illustrates the importance of having our names written in the book. Several years ago, she was asked to sing at the wedding of a very wealthy man. According to the invitation, the reception would be held on the top two floors of Seattle's Columbia Tower, the Northwest's tallest skyscraper. She and her husband, Roy, were excited about attending.

At the reception, waiters in tuxedos offered luscious hors d'oeuvres and exotic beverages. The bride and groom approached a beautiful glass and brass staircase that led to the top floor. Someone ceremoniously cut a satin ribbon draped across the bottom of the stairs. They announced the wedding feast was about to begin. Bride and groom ascended the stairs, followed by their guests.

At the top of the stairs, a maître d' with a bound book greeted the guests outside the doors.

"May I have your name, please?"

"I am Ruthanna Metzgar, and this is my husband, Roy."

He searched the M's.

"I'm not finding it. Would you spell it, please?"

Ruthanna spelled her name slowly. After searching the book, the maître d' looked up and said, "I'm sorry, but your name isn't here."

"There must be some mistake," Ruthanna replied. "I'm the singer. I sang for this wedding!"

The gentleman answered, "It doesn't matter who you are or what you did. Without your name in the book, you cannot attend the banquet."

He motioned to a waiter and said, "Show these people to the service elevator, please."

The Metzgars followed the waiter past beautifully decorated tables laden with shrimp, whole smoked salmon, and magnificent carved ice sculptures. Adjacent to the banquet area, an orchestra was preparing to perform, the musicians all dressed in dazzling white tuxedos.

The waiter led Ruthanna and Roy to the service elevator, ushered them in, and pushed G for the parking garage.

After locating their car and driving several miles in silence, Roy reached over and put his hand on Ruthanna's arm. "Sweetheart, what happened?"

"When the invitation arrived, I was busy," Ruthanna replied. "I never bothered to RSVP. Besides, I was the singer. Surely I could go to the reception without returning the RSVP!"

Ruthanna started to weep—not only because she had missed the most lavish banquet she'd ever been invited to, but also because she suddenly had a small taste of what it will be like someday for people as they stand before Christ and find their names are not written in the Lamb's Book of Life.

Throughout the ages, countless people have been too busy to respond to Christ's invitation to his wedding banquet. Many assume that the good they've done—perhaps attending church, being baptized, singing in the choir, or helping in a soup kitchen—will be enough to gain entry to heaven. But people who do not respond to Christ's invitation to forgive their sins are people whose names aren't written in the Lamb's Book of Life. To be denied entrance to heaven's wedding banquet will not just mean going down the service elevator to the garage. It will mean being cast outside into Hell, forever.

In that day, no explanation or excuse will count. All that will matter is whether our names are written in the book. If they're not, we'll be turned away.

Have you said yes to Christ's invitation to join Him at the wedding feast and spend eternity with Him in His house? If so, you have reason to rejoice—heaven's gates will be open to you.

If you have been putting off your response, your RSVP, or if you presume that you can enter heaven without responding to Christ's invitation, one day you will deeply regret it.[1]

This is a rather sobering thought, isn't it? Over many years of leading or co-leading Christian groups of various sizes with people of diverse backgrounds in and outside the church environment, I am sad about how few individuals have even thought about where they might spend eternity. Do you know how long that is? Most people I talk to seem to fixate on just enjoying the "here and now" with little thought about the future, so they probably have no assurance of heaven.

Have you thought about what might happen to you when you die? So many times when I ask people that question, they say they haven't given it much thought. I recognize this question may make some people squirm and perhaps feel overwhelmed when they realize they don't know. If that is you, I encourage you to press in more to discover the truth about it rather than passively ignoring the question.

Even among the Christians I've met, so many are not enjoying the benefits of surrender and obedience to God, leading them to experience an empowered, victorious life. For me, this has been a lengthy journey, and I long to share with you my failures, revelations, and experiences.

I have found that those most interested in controlling what happens in their life and having their needs met are missing the purpose God has for them. They think they are experiencing the "happy life," but there is so much more "left on the table" waiting for them to experience. They don't know what they don't know.

I have been blessed to be under incredible teaching and Bible study most of my adult life. While I've had ups and downs like everyone else, I have learned and experienced so much that I can't wait to share with you.

Especially if you are not sure about your spiritual condition and absolutely certain you will go to heaven, this book is for you. You *can* experience a fulfilled life of certainty no matter what storms, valleys, or mountains you might encounter. It's important to know that even though you may feel you are experiencing a tsunami in your life now, if it were not for storms, there would be no rainbows. You *can* have a remarkable peace that surpasses all understanding. Life is a journey, and this book is the starting point on your roadmap to victory.

If you are a Christ-follower and you wish for your friends or family to understand the truths of eternity but are not sure how to explain what they are missing, this book should help. Maybe you can learn how to share the truth with them so they will understand, or perhaps you can share this book with them. I've tried to make it very clear what it takes to experience eternal life in heaven. I long to take as many with me as possible!

I write like I talk, and have written this book as if you and I are close friends (which I hope we are someday). I hope this gives me permission to be honest and straightforward—speaking the truth in love as I write. ☺ I envision us curled up on my family room sofa with a cup of hot chocolate. As we watch a roaring fire in my fireplace on a chilly autumn night, I will share my heart with you while we discuss our future and the essential things in life.

# CHAPTER 1

## ARE YOU SURE YOU'LL GO TO HEAVEN WHEN YOU DIE?

I would think everyone would love to feel like they are winners in the game of life. We all like to believe we are pretty much at the top of our game, enjoying life at its fullest. As a Christ-follower, that will look different than the average person who does not yet know Christ. You see, knowing Christ—personally—changes our life for eternity, and eternity is a long time. Eternity matters. It matters a lot!

One fact we can count on is we all will die a physical death someday, and yes, our spirit *will* live forever, and forever is a *long* time. The question is, where? There are only two destinations: heaven and hell. If you are not going to one, you will go to the other. Jesus said, "Whoever is not with Me is against Me" (Luke 11:23).

What is your destination? You may say, "Wait a minute, I have nothing against God; I just don't think He has any relevance in my life. I'm basically a good person, so why wouldn't I go to heaven?"

That is the lie Satan would love for you to believe. God is pretty clear in His Word, that if you are not "all in" with Him, you are His enemy. Hang on, and I'll explain. If you believe there are many paths to heaven and being a Christ-follower is only one of several ways, stick with me here. I will discuss that as well.

There is no "in-between," and no, death is not just a matter of our candle blowing out. If you were to study every culture as far back as you could go in time, you would find a universal belief in an afterlife. Most people believe there is a great place for good people and a bad place for evil people. Of course, some will tell you they think there is no afterlife, and our life just ends when we die. That's a state of denial. Eternity has been implanted in the heart of humanity.

The problem is we believe a misconception of what heaven is and what to expect. We don't think we can know what awaits us when we die; however, the Bible gives us a lot of clues. I have two resources at the end of this book that give a lot more detail about heaven. Randy Alcorn's *Heaven* is based on exhaustive research and provides an extensive description—as much as we could know without having a personal tour. Chip Ingram's *The Real Heaven,* while also based on extensive biblical research, is much shorter and more of a summary. If we have a true understanding of what heaven is like, it should affect how we live our life now. A faulty view of heaven will lead to a wasted life here on earth.

I will not try to describe heaven or hell here because that is beyond the scope of this book. I think of an abbreviated definition of heaven as "a literal paradise with a constant experience of unconditional love." At the same time, we can describe hell as "an eternal punishment of inconsolable grief and unrelenting torment."

We *do* know some things. We know from Jesus's words in the Bible that heaven and hell are real places. God is in heaven, and Jesus is at His right hand. Those who have died before us who loved Jesus are there. If we are a Christ-follower, our names are written in the Book of Life I mentioned earlier which means we get to go there. Just know for now you definitely want to make sure you end up in heaven. We are talking about "eternity" here with no way out, and that's a *long* time for regret.

Speaking of hell, you might ask, if God is such a good and loving God, why would He create and send people to such a place of agony or torment? Well, besides being a God of "love," He also is a God of "justice." We all know people we hope will get justice because of the heinous things they have done. Of course, we don't think of ourselves necessarily as needing that kind of justice. However, any sin (it doesn't have to be monstrous or scandalous) will separate us from a holy God who cannot look upon sin. He provided a way to escape that justice, and that is what I will discuss in this book. Once we die, we have already made our choice, and we cannot change our minds or our ways. The time to settle and straighten that out is *now.* Every breath we breathe is a gift from God, and He does not promise us tomorrow.

Many, I'm afraid have a diminished view of life because of a distorted view of God. Please keep an open mind and hear me out. This booklet is a short, quick read and well worth your time. I want to help you understand how you can know your destination. Your mission, should you choose to accept it, is to carefully consider all that I share in these pages and take the necessary steps to secure your place in heaven.

Please understand my heart in this. I am taking the time and effort to share this with you, not because I know it all or feel in any way superior to you. I am far from perfect; I certainly don't have it all together, and I have baggage just like everyone else. I am writing this because the "life-changing" love of Christ I have experienced compels me to share this "life-giving" message to everyone I can. Even though I don't know you, I hope to see you in heaven!

I was listening to a webinar by an author coach the other day, and she gave us an exercise. She told us to think about how the word "comedy" related to our book. Because of the

*God bases where we spend eternity on choices and decisions we make now while we are alive.*

seriousness of this topic, I couldn't relate to that word; but then she gave us another one. She said, "Try the word 'horror.'"

I immediately thought of the horror of millions of people going to hell instead of heaven because they don't know what they don't know, or possibly because of pride, or a moral issue of which they don't want to let go. Please, don't let any excuses stand in the way of hearing and responding to the truth.

*If you wanted nothing to do with God while on earth, then He will not force you to live with Him in eternity.*

God ultimately decides our destination for us, but He bases where we spend eternity on choices and decisions we make *now* while we are alive. Just realize if you wanted nothing to do with God while on earth (making Him your enemy), then He will not force you to live with Him in eternity. His response will be, "Thy will be done." You will be separated from Him and any godly influence forever. God *is* love and the author of life. He is the Creator and sustainer of anything and everything good, so if you are separated from Him (by your choice), you will be separated from anything good - *forever.*

## HOW LONG IS FOREVER?

That's kind of hard to wrap your head around, isn't it? I realize I am about to compare time and space, which are two different things, but I hope you can grasp the scope of this comparison. Suppose you live to be 100. Think about your life representing a grain of sand and think of each grain of sand being another lifetime of 100 years each. Think about all the grains of sand on all the beaches and deserts of the world. Even that quantity is finite, but think of all the grains of sand making up eternity.

Here's another comparison. It takes at least ninety-three billion light-years to travel across our universe. Yes, that's "billion" with a "b." More stars are in space than grains of sand on the earth. Suppose your lifetime represented a helium balloon floating up into that universe—the universe representing eternity. I hope you get the point. Eternity is "forever" and is longer than we can conceptualize.

Our time on this earth is but a hiccup in light of eternity. In the book of James—in the New Testament, the author tells us that our life is but a "mist" (James 4:14). What happens and where we go when we die is by far the most significant issue in our life, but few give it much thought while we "eat, drink, and make merry."

Jesus talked a lot about heaven and hell, but we don't talk about it much, which is a shame because it is *so* important. I think we are often afraid of upsetting someone, but I am more concerned about your salvation and where you spend eternity than I am of offending you. I hope I do not sound too blunt here, but this is too important for me to shirk the truth. I will tell you right now there is

> *There is **nothing** more important in your life than your relationship with God.*

**nothing** more important in your life than your relationship with God. If you don't have one, or you feel far from God, you need to pay very close attention to all that follows.

A burden I have been carrying for a very long time is I am afraid there will be millions of astonished and distraught people when they die and find themselves in hell when they thought all along they were going to heaven. Their confusion is probably because of a lack of information or misconception of what a true Christian is and what it takes to get into heaven.

Millions of people probably think they will go to heaven, but unless they accept Jesus Christ as their personal Lord and Savior, and allow

Christ to transform them, they are destined to hell. Many, I fear, are self-deceived, and unfortunately, numerous churches contribute to that deception by what and how they teach.

This is something you do *not* want to get wrong. You can get many things in this world wrong that have no lasting impact, but where you spend eternity has *everlasting* significance, and it is *extremely* important you understand the truth.

If you are not positively sure you will go to heaven, please, I beg you to stick with me here, as I explain as thoroughly and as succinctly as I can, what a true Christian is and is not. I will take my time with this because I want to be sure you get it. I want to see you in heaven!

Even if you know without a doubt you are a Christ-follower, I implore you to read through this next section anyway as it may help you identify some deceived people in your life. Maybe you can discover a way to help guide them on the right path so they can know Jesus.

*The good news is heaven is possible for anyone, and you can know you are going there.*

He gave the Great Commission to all believers, and surely you want to share the good news of the gospel to those who don't know or understand it. Just like you would never hoard the cure for cancer if you had it, why would you hoard your knowledge of the cure for unending destruction and what it takes to experience the alternative—eternal life in heaven?

## WHY ARE WE HERE ON THIS EARTH?

Colossians 1:16 says we were created *by* Jesus and *for* Jesus. We were created with a God-shaped vacuum in our heart, which remains empty until He fills it by *our* invitation only. We may try to fill this emptiness with any number of things until we realize *He* is the missing element. All of humanity experiences a desire to fill that space. Still, many try to fill it with something, anything *they* think will make them happy.

So many of those choices are incredibly destructive. Most of us have at least felt a "spiritual" need. That is why so many different religions have cropped up over the centuries. To embrace Christianity, we have to believe in God, accept Jesus's sacrificial death for us, and face our sins, which is not too popular. He won't force Himself on anyone, so we have to make a choice.

Christianity is not a religion, but a relationship with a personal God with whom we can have a deep connection. Jesus created us to live *for* Him, and He wants a relationship *with* us but cannot and will not as long as we put ourselves first.

> *Christianity is not a religion, but a relationship with a personal God with whom we can have a deep connection.*

A Gallup poll taken in June of 2016[1] showed that 89 percent of Americans believe in God, which shows a decline from previous decades. The percentage keeps going down. That may seem like a lot, but let me warn you that while believing in God is a good starting point, just academically believing there is a God does not guarantee anyone eternity with Him. According to the Bible, we cannot *know* God unless we *experience* Him. Unfortunately, most people don't understand that. There is a lot more to it than superficial head knowledge. The Bible teaches that even Satan believes in God, and he trembles.

An earlier poll revealed that for every one American who believed they were going to hell, 120 thought they were going to heaven.[2] According to the Bible, we don't automatically go to heaven. Unfortunately, we are all born with a sinful nature, and the default destination is hell. That's the bad news. The good news is heaven *is*

*We cannot know God unless we experience Him.*

possible for *anyone,* and you can *know* you are going there. If you aren't sure, please read on. The assurance of your salvation lies ahead if you embrace what I share with you. First John 5:13 tells us: "I write these things to you who believe in the name of the Son of God, that you may know that you have eternal life."

# CHAPTER 2

## NOW LET'S LOOK AT THE WORD "CHRISTIAN"

Unfortunately, this word is very misunderstood, misused, and misconstrued so much that there is considerable confusion as to what it actually means. I will take quite a bit of time here to show what Scripture (the Holy Word of God) tells us what it takes to be a Christian. I based this whole book on Scripture because that is the inspired Word of God given to us for instruction. It is the "Truth" God spoke Himself through those He inspired to write it.

If you take issue with the Bible being the inspired Word of God, you need to read my book, *Forever is a Long Time to be Wrong,* where I explain more about how we know the Bible is true based on all kinds of evidence.

The urgency of getting this book to print was escalated recently as my husband officiated a "Celebration of Life" ceremony for his best friend of over fifty-five years who died from complications from Parkinson's and cancer. I know my husband, Bob, witnessed to John many times, sharing the good news of the gospel with him. He would tell him that he wanted to see him in heaven, and his friend would always say, "Well, you know I always try to do the right thing."

John was a retired FBI agent with a rich career being a SWAT team leader at one point and certainly lived a life of fidelity, bravery, and integrity—three things that exemplify an upstanding FBI agent. He did much to contribute to the safety of our nation by his service. Those who knew him would tell you he was 100 percent faithful to his wife and by the world's standards, considered a good husband, father, neighbor, and friend. However, he was in the category of those who believe by living a virtuous life and being a good person that God would honor his goodness with forgiveness for his failures and reward him with eternal life in heaven—even though he did not have a personal relationship with Christ.

Unfortunately, that is not what the Bible teaches about salvation and eternal life. Before we go into what the Bible says, I looked up "Christian" on dictionary.com[1], and as a noun, it means, "A person who believes in Jesus Christ and one whose life exemplifies the teachings of Christ."

That's a pretty good definition, but there is more to it than that, and the first part is lacking and could be misleading. Academic belief is not enough, as I will explain. A person also can imitate the life of someone they admire and unknowingly emulate Christian behavior to an extent without being a Christian.

> When we become a Christian, He comes to live inside us and desires to live His life through us in the person of the Holy Spirit.

The *Holman Bible Dictionary*[2] states, "A Christian is a believer of Christ, a follower committed to Christ." Our goal as a Christ-follower indeed is to be Christlike—to live a life that personifies Him in a way others see Christ in us and are drawn to Him. We are to be His hands and feet and even His mouthpiece—an extension of Him to those with whom we come into contact. We can do this because when we become a Christian, He comes to live inside us and desires to live His life through us in the person of the Holy Spirit.

## How Does Christ Come to Live Inside Us as the Holy Spirit?

This is difficult to grasp, but I will try to explain briefly in simple terms what the Trinity is—the three-in-one Godhead—one God in three forms with different functions. If you were to use math to explain it, the equation would *not* be 1+1+1=3, but 1x1x1=1. There is God the Father, God the Son, and God the Holy Spirit. The word "Tri" means three, and the word "unity" means one. God is only One—but in the form of three Persons who have the same essence of deity but different functions. Because they are three in one, we often use each name interchangeably.

Jesus was in the beginning with God, and He was God but left the glory of heaven to come to earth to save us from our sins by taking it upon Himself to receive God's wrath in our place. Then, when He went back to the Father after He rose from being dead, He sent the Holy Spirit to point us to Himself and empower us to fulfill God's will as He reveals it to us.

It was to our advantage that Jesus returned to the Father so that we could experience the power of the Holy Spirit in each of our lives when we turn our life over to Christ. He indwells the heart of every believer.

If your belief in Jesus Christ is purely academic, in that you just believe He lived and even died on the cross, Satan, the devil, believes that as well. He knows for sure Jesus existed and died on the cross. He even knows the purpose of Jesus's death was to be a sacrificial substitute for the sins of humanity. However, he has rejected that gift, and he shutters to think of the implications of Jesus's sacrifice. If you only believe in God/Jesus as a fact and have not accepted/received Jesus's life in exchange for yours, you do not have the Holy Spirit living inside you. You have not experienced the "exchanged life."

If you examine or study any religion other than Christianity, you will find the philosophy they teach and accept is that salvation is based on works. One is to strive to achieve status with God because of their good works. In these other "religions," there is the hope good works will outweigh the bad. The problem with that is there is never a guarantee God will accept them based on their performance. (Spoiler alert—He never accepts us based on our performance. Salvation is not something we can earn.)

The difference true Christianity offers is: Christ is the One who took the initiative and reached down to earth to save us because of His love for us. He is the initiator, the One who did all the work. We just have to believe and receive.

*Salvation is not something we can earn.*

These other religions leave too much to chance, and there is never any assurance if a person has "made it" or not. How does one know when they have ever done "enough?" They don't. Let's look at what the Bible tells us about what it takes to be a Christ-follower. That is the first step. We will start with Matthew 7:21–27:

> Not everyone who says to Me, 'Lord, Lord,' will enter the kingdom of heaven, but the one who does the will of My Father who is in heaven. On that day many will say to Me, 'Lord, Lord, did we not prophesy in your name, and cast out demons in your name, and do many mighty works in your name?' And then will I declare to them, 'I never knew you; depart from Me, you workers of lawlessness.'

> Everyone then who hears these words of mine and does them will be like a wise man who built his house on the rock. And the rain fell, and the floods came, and the winds blew and beat on that house, but it did not fall,

18

because it had been founded on the rock. And everyone who hears these words of mine and does not do them will be like a foolish man who built his house on the sand. And the rain fell, and the floods came, and the winds blew and beat against that house, and it fell, and great was the fall of it.

Earlier in that same chapter, Jesus tells us in verses 13 and 14 that there are only two options for a human being in light of eternity, "Enter by the narrow gate. For the gate is wide and the way is easy that leads to destruction, and those who enter by it are many. For the gate is narrow and the way is hard that leads to life, and those who find it are few."

My goal is to help you find the "narrow" way. What could be more tragic than to think you are "okay" and going to heaven when you die just because you didn't take eternity seriously enough to do your "due diligence" to listen, research, and learn all you can about it? If you or a loved one had some life-threatening illness, wouldn't you study and do exhaustive research to find out what to do to help and possibly cure the disease?

*We must recognize we are a sinner in need of a Savior.*

To enter through the narrow gate, we must deny ourselves and our self-righteousness. We must recognize we are a sinner in need of a Savior. We must repent, which means to make a U-turn from our habitual, sinful lifestyle, submit ourselves to Christ, and commit to obey and follow Him no matter what the cost. It means taking responsibility for our sins. Sin always produces loss. Every man is born with his back to God.

Repentance is simply a change of course—making an about-face. In fact, true repentance involves a dramatic and decisive radical change of heart and direction that will save us from disastrous consequences. We have not repented if we continue to habitually sin.

19

Some people, including my husband's friend, feel that becoming a Christian is too easy. The first step *is* easy because it was exclusively God's work. But Christ continually emphasized the difficulty of following Him.

Salvation is by grace alone (meaning it *is* a gift to receive), but implementation and discipleship are not easy at all. It calls for knowledge of the truth, repentance, submission to Christ as Lord, and a willingness to obey His will and Word. Don't worry, once you become a Christ-follower, you are no longer on your own, but have the Holy Spirit inside you to guide you, and He will provide what you need to experience God fully—and that is what a Christian is.

*Sin always produces loss. Every man is born with his back to God.*

# Chapter 3

## Let's Stop for a Minute and Talk about Sin

We as a race are so self-absorbed and selfish, and our heart is naturally wired to love sin and self-gratification and to follow our hearts. We would never admit it, but subconsciously we act as if the universe centers around us and whatever makes us happy.

What is sin exactly? *Dictionary.com*[1] states sin is "an immoral act considered to be a transgression against a divine law." I would add that sin is anything that displeases God or trying to get the "good" apart from God. It's trying to solve our problems and even save ourselves instead of relying on God's grace. *The Holman Bible Dictionary*[2] defines sin as: "Actions by which humans rebel against God, miss His purpose for their life, and surrender to the power of evil rather than to God." The Bible says we all are sinners: "for all have sinned and fall short of the glory of God" (Romans 3:23).

So...why do we sin? We sin because we want to. When we do something sinful, it is a result of a deeply rooted sinful affection.

To escape the grasp of sin in our lives, we must see and acknowledge it for what it is and not just call it a "mistake," a "bad habit," or a "weakness." We also must not blame others for our sin or let pride get in the way of

> *To escape the grasp of sin in our lives, we must see and acknowledge it for what it is and not just call it a "mistake," a "bad habit," or a "weakness."*

admitting our wrongdoing. The good news is God's grace abounds all the more to free us (Romans 5:20). He wants to forgive us.

Sin is much more than just an action; it's much bigger than that. It's a force or power that works on our hearts. It's the enemy at work against us. It is a result of listening to the wrong voice in our head. For too long, we have been plagued with feelings of inadequacy and insufficiency, thinking we just aren't good enough. That's the enemy talking. We know we are sinful and don't deserve to receive salvation in our current state. That's why we have such a hard time accepting the gift Jesus offers to us. It just seems too easy, and we would feel better if we could earn it.

The reason sin becomes an action is because it originally was an affection. In our original state, we only do what we want to do. According to David Bowden in his book, *Rewire Your Heart,* our wants run deeper than our wishes. If we want to change our *will* to sin, we must change our *desire* for sin. Passion wins out over preference."[3] What is your passion?

When we sin, it's because our heart wants to. We sin with our thoughts, words, or deeds because sin is in our hearts. Habitual sin is an addiction we must overcome. We cannot act apart from our affections. Our actions are unquestionably linked to our deepest desires. God wants those deepest wants and affections to be about Him so that He can truly change us.

*The reason sin becomes an action is because it originally was an affection.*

God hardwired us to follow our hearts; that's why to follow Him truly, it requires a new heart of obedience. Our hearts reveal who we actually are. Christianity is not so much about saying "no" to sin. It's more about loving God with all that we have. As He becomes the center of our affections, our desire to sin diminishes.

The truth about our sin is we lack trust and faith in God to carry out His promises. It is a lack of belief in His provision. An example is worry, which is the antithesis to faith. So the real root underlying our sin problem is unbelief, and that always comes before a lack of trust. That is our biggest battle and greatest sin besides pride, which is rooted in self-sufficiency.

*Our actions are unquestionably linked to our deepest desires.*

The problem originates in our hearts. Therefore, we need a "heart change." The battle against sin is a battle for our hearts—a fight for our affections. We must rewire our hearts and redirect our affections to experience God's fullness in our lives as we prepare for eternity.

## FALSE BELIEFS THAT RESULT IN FUTILE PATHWAYS TO HEAVEN

Unfortunately, many take the "wide" road, and plenty of false prophets are out there, enabling those who will listen. In Matthew 7, verses 15-20, Jesus warns us:

Beware of false prophets, who come to you in sheep's clothing but inwardly are ravenous wolves. You will recognize them by their fruits. Are grapes gathered from thornbushes, or figs from thistles? So, every healthy tree bears good fruit, but the diseased tree bears bad fruit. A healthy tree cannot bear bad fruit, nor can a diseased tree bear good fruit. Every tree that does not bear good fruit is cut down and thrown into the fire. Thus you will recognize them by their fruits.

When Jesus said these things, He was speaking to the Pharisees—the prideful religious leaders. The sad thing is, they had no relationship with God or Christ. They were religious (meaning they were devout and even faithful to the "law"), but they did not understand anything about God's grace. They were lost—on the wide path. They had a form of godliness, but without the reality of it and were thus self-deceived.

It is a tragedy that anyone from any religion should perish; but what is frightening is many "so-called" Christians think that by a variety of things they do, they are on their way to heaven. But they have been deceived.

*The problem originates in our hearts. Therefore, we need a "heart change."*

Some pastors are even leading their congregations astray, probably not intentionally, but because they have been deceived themselves about their true spiritual condition. Many are trying to appease those emerging in a changing culture. The problem with that is, God and nothing about Him or His Word ever changes or was ever intended to change. His Word, moral law, and truths are eternal, and He is immutable (never changing).

There is a tendency in today's society for individuals to change their minds and accept different ideas of what they consider to be right or wrong. They base this circular thinking on opinions coming from sinful hearts influenced by cultural changes and what seems to be popular and trending as acceptable in society at the time.

We can ignore God's spiritual and moral laws, but we do so at our own risk. His commands are timeless, and He created them for our own good—to protect and save us from much heartache and even death if we follow them as He intended.

I could give many examples, but one would be adultery. God forbids it in Scripture because He knows how devastating and heartbreaking it is not only to the spouse who is the victim, but to everyone close to that couple (family members, friends, and the church body). This behavior breaks His laws that He created for our good. When we sin, it never just affects us; it affects all those around us. When we ignore His laws in favor of our poor choices, we rob ourselves of the delights

*When we sin, we choose to live by our standards other than by God's perfect laws, which come with benefits and rewards rather than heartache.*

He has in store for us. When we sin, we choose to live by our standards other than by God's perfect laws, which come with benefits and rewards rather than heartache.

Culture does not displace them; neither do circumstances nullify them. Yes, laws have been made to legalize some things that go against the Bible's commands, but we have no moral right to change anything God has put into place through His Word. So we may have a legal right to some things but not the moral or ethical right according to the Word of God.

It is crucial for us to know what the Bible says and to understand it, so we will know when we are being taught fallacies or even half-truths. Many individuals have no idea of what the Bible teaches, the truths of the gospel, or the need for salvation. Many teachings have been watered down and trivialized to where a meaningful explanation of redemption is lost.

Many people today believe in God and maybe even Jesus, but are utterly absent of any divine life, any real knowledge of God, or salvation. Tragically, many are entirely unaware but comfortable in their deception.

What is so heartbreaking is many non-believers are active in the Christian community, maybe even serving in the church, rubbing shoulders with Christians, but have never had a life change—they did not allow Christ to transform them. But because of their loyalty in their attendance and participation, they have a false sense of assurance that they are Christians. Does that sound or look at all familiar?

They have learned the lingo, maybe even know a few Bible verses. They have gotten caught up in what I would call a "Cultural Christianity," which is not being a Christian at all except in their minds. By being "so" involved in religious activity, they have let themselves become deceived into thinking that is all it takes to be a Christian.

Unfortunately, that will not get them into heaven. They would fail at self-examination. Quite possibly, well-meaning Christians have befriended those who like to associate with them, and continue to affirm these folks but stop short of actually drawing them into serious conversations about their faith. Of course, we are to love and accept everyone; but if we really cared, we would, at some point, share the truth of the gospel with these people. This lack of openness is tragic because these individuals are living a lie and don't even know it.

If anyone says they aren't sure if they are a Christian, there is a good chance they are not. If truly you are a Christ-follower, you know it. You could be experiencing a temporary temptation to doubt because of an attack by Satan causing uncertainty, but generally, you know if you have repented and made a commitment to Christ.

You *could* be a Christian but living a defeated life by succumbing to self-sufficiency. That is so easy to happen when we find life getting in the way sometimes, and we forget what is available to us through Christ, and we forget to make Him Lord as we press on in our efforts.

# CHAPTER 4

## BUT I'M A GOOD PERSON

The biggest lie the world buys into is what I mentioned earlier, that God would accept someone into heaven simply because they are a good person, and God wouldn't send a good person to hell, right? I know many good, ethical individuals who do a lot of humanitarian things and don't see a need for a Savior because they don't see themselves as sinners. They see themselves as "good" people. They honestly think people in general are inherently good. God tells us, though, in Romans 3:10, "None is righteous, no not one." Also, in Romans 3:23, we find, "for all have sinned and fall short of the glory of God."

Jesus came to save the ungodly, and if we don't see ourselves as sinners needing salvation, then we cannot receive it. We all are broken people who need a Savior. The more we realize how far we fall short, the closer we are to being saved as we look to Jesus to save us.

Some believe and agree with what they understand about biblical morality, so falsely think that should justify their entrance into heaven. Our virtue or "goodness" we see in ourselves can actually be a deterrent because it keeps us from seeing our need for change.

*We all are broken people who need a Savior.*

Unfortunately, nothing I just mentioned brings about salvation. As I said earlier, Satan believes in God and knows the Bible inside and out,

27

upside down and backward, but he certainly isn't saved. Probably unknowingly, these people are trying to get to heaven through the wide road rather than the narrow gate Jesus talks about in Matthew. Qualifications for entering the narrow gate are:

- Recognition, confession, and repentance for sin
- Brokenness
- Humility
- Submission/surrender to the Lordship of Christ
- Obedience to the Word of God no matter what

Jesus, who was sinless, traded His righteousness for our sin and took on the wrath of God against sin on our behalf and died in our place. Romans 5:8 tells us, "but God shows His love for us in that while we were still sinners, Christ died for us."

## EXCHANGE GOOD FOR RIGHTEOUSNESS

This exchange of our life for His put to rest the punishment of our sins past, present, and future so we could spend eternity in heaven with Him. Second Corinthians 5:21 says, "For our sake He made Him to be sin who knew no sin, so that in Him we might become the righteousness of God."

*Jesus knows our sins very well; however, He did not come to rub them in, but to rub them out.*

In this inconceivable exchange, God took all of humanity's sins and heaped them on His righteous, sinless Son. For the first time, Jesus was separated from God since God cannot look upon sin and had to turn His back on Him. The holy Son of God could have done nothing more marvelous or miraculous for us than this. Experiencing His Father's wrath in our place (and we are talking

28

about all the sins of everyone—past, present, and future) would have been more agonizing for Him to endure than even the physical suffering, which was so visible and horrendous.

Jesus knows our sins very well; however, He did not come to rub them in, but to rub them out. He did not come to condemn or shame us, but to save and change us. Why did Jesus die for you? Because He wants to spend eternity with you. Isn't that mind-blowing love!

This incredible act of love is what drew me to Christ when I was a child. My mom used to read me Bible stories at bedtime, and I was so overwhelmed with the crucifixion story that I repeatedly asked her to read that one to me over and over again. I could not comprehend that someone would take the punishment I deserved and die for me in such a horrific death so that I could live forever with God in heaven.

I didn't even understand the wrath of God or human rejection at that point, but I certainly understood physical pain. How could I *not* love someone like that? I have loved Jesus ever since.

Have I always been obedient to Him once I started studying the Bible and learning how a Christian was supposed to look and act? Absolutely not! Like anyone else, I have struggled to surrender particular weaknesses and vulnerabilities to Him.

In fact, for a while, I thought I was doing pretty well in my walk with the Lord when I would compare myself to others I knew—even godly friends. Then I realized with the help of the Holy Spirit (that is a big part of His job—to convict us when we are wrong), I was comparing myself to the wrong people. I was supposed to compare myself to Christ, not other sinners.

*He did not come to condemn or shame us, but to save and change us.*

*I have discovered only Jesus can satisfy our deepest desires.*

I will say the more serious I have become in following Christ and asking Him to show me what it looks like to totally surrender to Him, the more the "sin quotient" in my life has substantially diminished. I'm a slow learner, and I still fail at times, but I have finally learned what it takes to live a victorious Christian life, and I want to give you a taste of that within these pages. There is nothing like it, and I want more than anything for you to experience it!

As I progress in my Christian walk, I have discovered only Jesus can satisfy our deepest desires. We fulfill our fundamental longing to live with God by receiving His grace as He reshapes our twisted aspirations to earn His approval through our works. We can now accomplish our deepest desire by merely resting in Him and what He has already done. We *were* saved by works—His!

When we accept that indescribable gift of love, God then sees us through the blood Christ shed for us, and even though we still sin at times, He no longer sees us as sinners, but as righteous. I know it sounds unimaginable, doesn't it? God works in such mysterious ways.

Just before He died, Jesus said, "It is finished" (John 19:30). That is actually a legal term for when a debt has been paid off. So, He literally meant, "Paid in Full." This finished work means we need to add nothing to what He accomplished on the cross for our salvation.

*He bought eternity for us by giving up His life. Isn't that amazing?*

You may have heard the term, "He paid the ransom." That means He paid for us with His life. It is in Matthew 20:28, "Even as the Son of Man came not to be served but to serve, and to give His life as a ransom for many."

Titus 3:5-7 says, "He saved us, not because of works done by us in righteousness, but according to His own mercy, by the washing of regeneration and renewal of the Holy Spirit, whom He poured out on us richly through Jesus Christ our Savior, so that being justified by His grace we might become heirs according to the hope of eternal life."

> *When we accept Jesus Christ as Lord of our life, we trade our worthless sin for the incredible work of His righteousness.*

What was the ransom He paid for us? His life. He gave up His life. He died in our place, taking on God's wrath so that we wouldn't have to. We are now heirs of eternal life with Him. He bought eternity for us by giving up His life. Isn't that amazing? That is what this is all about.

We are no longer slaves to sin but servants of Christ. "We know that our old self was crucified with Him in order that the body of sin might be brought to nothing, so that we would no longer be enslaved to sin" (Romans 6:6). The lifestyle change and "end of life assurance" from that ownership change is incomprehensible.

Jesus is our source for righteousness and should be our *only* pursuit. When we accept Jesus Christ as Lord of our life, we trade our worthless sin for the incredible work of His righteousness.

# CHAPTER 5

## A RELATIONSHIP WITH GOD REQUIRES SURRENDER

What God wants most from us is our heart, our inner man, and our submission to *His* will, which is always in our best interest. He wants to be in a relationship with us. He wants our obedience above all sacrifices or works. He wants us to relinquish control of our lives, thoughts, and actions to Him who can do so much more for our good and the good of others through us than we ever could do on our own. The very best way we can love God is to surrender our lives fully to Him in obedience to His Word and demonstrate we are "all in" for Him. That's ultimately what God wants from us—to trade our sinful life for His righteousness.

I will spell out several scenarios below of erroneous beliefs. While they are not exhaustive, I wonder if you might find yourself in one of these categories. Some people may have attended an event earlier in their life where they were caught up in the emotion of the moment and believed in God and what Jesus did on the cross. They may look back on that as confirmation they are a Christian. They may have even prayed a prayer. Only God knows if that took root. Maybe it did, perhaps not. The fruit of their life should be the indicator. What does their current character and lifestyle reveal?

> *That's ultimately what God wants from us— to trade our sinful life for His righteousness.*

33

To repeat as Matthew 7:18 tells us, "A healthy tree cannot bear bad fruit, nor can a diseased tree bear good fruit." And Matthew 12:33 tells us, "...the tree is known by its fruit," so we know the quality of the fruit tells us something about the root. If the fruit is unhealthy, it comes from an unhealthy root. If God is to get to the root of our life, He must be able to get to the root of our heart, which is our affections.

> *If God is to get to the root of our life, He must be able to get to the root of our heart, which is our affections.*

Speaking of fruit, regarding the root of your heart, here's some "fruit" for thought. When you squeeze a lemon, what comes out? Lemon juice, right? What happens when you are squeezed? Just wondering—since it will reveal what is inside.

Are you familiar with the parable of the seeds and the different kinds of soil Jesus told in Matthew 13:3-8?

> A sower went out to sow. And as he sowed, some seeds fell along the path, and the birds came and devoured them. Other seeds fell on rocky ground, where they did not have much soil, and immediately they sprang up, since they had no depth of soil, but when the sun rose they were scorched. And since they had no root, they withered away. Other seeds fell among thorns, and the thorns grew up and choked them. Other seeds fell on good soil and produced grain, some a hundredfold, some sixty, some thirty.

He then explains the parable in verses 18-23:

Hear then the parable of the sower: When anyone hears the word of the kingdom and does not understand it, the evil one comes and snatches away what has been sown in his heart. This is what was sown along the path. As for what was sown on rocky ground, this is the one who hears the word and immediately receives it with joy, yet he has no root in himself, but endures for a while, and when tribulation or persecution arises on account of the word, immediately he falls away. As for what was sown among thorns, this is the one who hears the word, but the cares of the world and the deceitfulness of riches choke the word, and it proves unfruitful. As for what was sown on good soil, this is the one who hears the word and understands it. He indeed bears fruit and yields, in one case a hundredfold, in another sixty, and in another thirty.

Let me explain this even more simply. If God's Words fall on deaf ears because of doubts, lack of interest, or distractions, it cannot take hold of your heart. If your heart is like the shallow soil on top of rocky ground, the truth cannot penetrate your heart enough to make a difference in your life. If your heart is like the thorny soil, it means you are easily distracted by the world in pursuit of earthly pleasures, which will prevent God's Word from taking root to produce any righteousness. A heart like the good soil will apply the word it receives and will produce good fruit. This is the kind of heart God desires in us because the fruit from it will be a Christlike life, which should be the goal of every believer.

Unfortunately, many people fall in one of the first three categories, never having truly become a committed Christ-follower. A story or an experience may have moved them, but maybe redemption did not take place. They did not actually experience a lasting heart change. They consider themselves to be Christians, but their lives have produced no fruit.

Many may have been brought up in the church, maybe attended with their parents, learned a lot about God, know many Bible stories, may have sung in the choir, served as an usher or greeter, and even taught Sunday school. Although they feel accepted and saved by association, they may never have made a personal commitment to Jesus.

> *If God is to get to the root of our life, He must be able to get to the root of our heart, which is our affections.*

Unfortunately, we cannot gain Christ through osmosis, and God has no grandchildren. We cannot get into heaven, riding on the coattails of our parents or friends. If you were born into and brought up in a Christian home, that does not make you a Christian any more than being brought up in a garage makes you a car. We must make our own decision whether or not to follow Christ and submit our life to Him.

Then there are the hypocrites. We all know those. They *could* be deceived, but they usually are deceivers themselves. If you are a Christian, most probably, you have been called a hypocrite at some point by outsiders. This group of people has been the most damaging to the church and the Christian community by posing as Christians when their words, actions, and attitudes suggest they probably are not.

Those of us who *are* Christians need to be very careful to "walk the talk," or else we could be guilty of hypocrisy ourselves, saying one thing but acting differently. We all fall short and could be accused of hypocrisy if humility and transparency are not part of our witness. Those guilty of hypocrisy certainly are not in a good place, and Jesus surely is not their "Lord," at least at the moment.

If you look closely, you will not see spiritual fruit in the life of a hypocrite. They don't look much if any different than those in the world (non-believers), and yet because they call themselves Christians, they have given Christianity a bad name. To outsiders, they have made all of us guilty by association.

> *If you were born into and brought up in a Christian home, that does not make you a Christian any more than being brought up in a garage makes you a car.*

How can we identify and help those who are deceived, whether or not they know it? Usually, these individuals are looking more for the blessings, experiences, healings, etc. that are the byproducts of the faith, not in Christ Himself.

They do not consume themselves with the awesomeness of God—of His holiness, the wonder of His glory, the honor due to Him, or the beauty and magnificence of Christ. They are not consumed with obedience, surrender to Him, or serving or submitting to Him with the honor and love He so deserves. They don't experience the joy of exalting Him through worship, proclaiming Him as Lord, and confessing Him as Savior.

They are more interested in what they can get in blessings and byproducts of being attached to Him like good feelings, a spiritual high, healing, or prosperity. These people also are usually more committed to a church or a denomination than Scripture because it is very likely more of a social thing for them.

Do you know someone more interested in theology as an academic interest than for personal holiness and worship? That should cause some concern. Do you know anyone who seems to always be "stuck" on one point of quirky theology?

## GOD'S GRACE DOES NOT MINIMIZE OUR NEED TO CONTINUALLY REPENT AND OBEY

Maybe you know someone who is over-indulgent about grace and lacks remorse. If someone is over-indulgent in their sins, and defends the way they conduct their life and lives a certain way because of a super, permissive grace lacking repentance, brokenness, or humility, it might be you see someone who is deceived.

A true Christian has ongoing brokenness—a continuous recognition that they fall short. A true Christian is always confessing their sins, consequently always experiencing forgiveness. Then some see God as a means to their own ends—a cosmic vending machine—who will grant all their requests, often expecting prosperity. I'm sorry, but that is *not* Christianity. We need to help those people understand *true* Christianity. "For the time is coming when people will not endure sound teaching, but having itching ears they will accumulate for themselves teachers to suit their own passions, and will turn away from listening to the truth and wander off into myths. As for you, always be sober-minded, endure suffering, do the work of an evangelist, fulfill your ministry" (2 Timothy 4:3–5).

*It's through the study of Scripture that we learn the heart of God.*

Often these folks say they want to commit themselves to God, but they seem to have no interest in studying His Word. Studying Scripture will produce personal growth and holiness in our lives, which should expand our worship. It's through the study of Scripture that we learn the heart of God. Profession without possession is the tragedy of all tragedies.

Some people's faith is so shallow they think they are saved before even realizing they are lost. They may also call Jesus "Lord," not understanding that by calling Him that, that means *He* is in charge. A person must recognize they are a sinner and be truly repentant of their current state to even desire a cleansing from God.

By reading His Word, we learn it says we are to confess our sins, repent, and embrace Jesus as our only hope of salvation. Then it says we are to deny ourselves, take up our cross daily, and follow Him (See Matthew 16:24). We are to count the cost of following Him. While salvation is free for us, it cost Jesus His life; and we need to take that very seriously. Prioritizing our relationship with Christ–putting Him in front and center of our life must become our passion.

> *Prioritizing our relationship with Christ–putting Him in front and center of our life must become our passion.*

Depending on one's current life status and cultural situation, there may be a tremendous cost, even persecution for making that kind of decision–to become a fully devoted follower of Christ. We must weigh that, count the cost, and be willing to submit and sacrifice whatever is necessary to accept the ransom Jesus paid for us. We are told that all who live godly lives in the name of Jesus at some point will suffer persecution of some sort. We need to realize if the *unbelieving world* has nothing to say *against* us, *Jesus* may have nothing to say *for* us. We *must* stand up for our convictions.

How are we to overcome persecution? Remember the words of Christ: "If the world hates you, know that it has hated Me before it hated you" (John 15:18). "In the world you will have tribulation. But take heart; I have overcome the world" (John 16:33).

Paul, a follower of Christ and New Testament writer, testifies that though persecuted, the Lord was always with him, strengthened him, and delivered him out of all his persecutions and afflictions. (1 Corinthians 4:8-10) Yes, following Jesus requires sacrifice, but it is well worth it, and the reward is endless and comes with eternal significance.

> *A gift a gift isn't until one receives it.*

God does not wish that anyone would perish. That is why He sent His Son, His one and only beloved Son into this world—to save all who were lost. But it is a gift with conditions we must meet and accept. A gift isn't a gift until one receives it. We are all God's creation, but we are not His children until we are willing to call Him "Father." He must become our Lord and Savior.

We know from John 3:16-18 that God loves the whole world He created, "For God so loved the world, that He gave His only Son, that whoever believes in Him should not perish but have eternal life. For God did not send His Son into the world to condemn the world, but in order that the world might be saved through Him. Whoever believes in Him is not condemned, but whoever does not believe is condemned already, because he has not believed in the name of the only Son of God."

He shows love to those who love and obey Him. Our God, who is full of grace, is very generous with the love He gives every person, but He reserves the right to demonstrate His loving mercy and blessing to those who are obedient to Him. Jesus says the same thing in John 14:21: "Whoever has My commands and keeps them, he it is who loves Me. And he who loves Me will be loved by My Father, and I will love him and manifest Myself to him."

> *God gave us His very best when He gave us His Son. The least we can do is give Him our highest devotion!*

40

God gave us His very best when He gave us His Son. The least we can do is give Him our highest devotion!

Let's clear up some possible misconceptions. We don't become a Christian just by what we *say*, but also what we *do* because of what is going on in our heart—I don't mean we achieve it by works. Don't misunderstand me on that. There is *nothing* we can ever do to *earn* our salvation. Ephesians 2:8-9 tells us: "For by grace you have been saved through faith. And this is not your own doing; it is the gift of God, not a result of works, so that no one may boast."

*The only "work" that can save us is the work of believing in what Jesus did to accomplish our salvation.*

The only "work" that can save us is the work of believing in what Jesus did to accomplish our salvation: "This is the work of God, that you believe in Him whom He has sent" (John 6:29). And to those who believe in their heart, God's promise stands firm: "To all who did receive Him, who believed in His name, He gave the right to become children of God" (John 1:12).

The "believe" and "receive" here goes way beyond intellectual understanding and assent. That is the point I am trying to make. It is talking about accepting all that comes with believing in Jesus and His sacrificial death. It's about repentance, obedience, and relinquishing control. It's about "dying" to self.

*God promises to add blessing in the lives of those who love and obey Him.*

God promises to add blessing in the lives of those who love and obey Him. What God wants is contrition, and if there is no remorse, there is not full repentance. We must, according to Romans 10:9-10, profess Jesus as Lord "because, if you confess with your mouth that Jesus is Lord and believe in your heart that

41

God raised Him from the dead, you will be saved. For with the heart one believes and is justified, and with the mouth one confesses and is saved."

We cannot make that type of admission without the help of the Holy Spirit who draws us to Christ. Confession never fails to bring a blessing. David tells us "a broken and contrite heart, O God, You will not despise" (Psalm 51:17).

Many sinners are sorry for their sins, but the sorrow is because they cannot continue in sin. They repent with hearts that are not broken. Salvation doesn't come simply to those who *only* profess it or speak of belief. Just giving lip service doesn't count. Empty words come from empty hearts. It's not the "sayers" who are saved; it's the doers.

*What God wants is contrition, and if there is no remorse, there is not full repentance.*

By this, I mean saving faith cannot be a mere intellectual exercise without a commitment to active obedience. Genuine faith produces obedience. God calls us to live, stand, and walk by faith. Once we accept Jesus Christ into our hearts as our Lord and Savior, besides resting in Him, His promises and truths, we have a responsibility to obey His Word. The way we live should reflect that change.

As I mentioned earlier, we can know a tree by its fruit. If you look back at Matthew 7:21-23, where Jesus tells those calling Him "Lord" that He never knew them, He referred to them as "workers of lawlessness." He is saying He never had a relationship of any kind with them.

He is referring here to hypocrites—professing Christ while living a sinful lifestyle. Doing good deeds for the wrong motives will get you the same response. Profession has no value if it stands alone. We must repent with a sincere desire to turn our life over to Christ. The true evidence of repentance is a changed life.

Let's be clear that just saying a "sinner's" prayer to gain salvation is not a "Get out of hell free" card. Jesus knows your heart even better than you do, and if you are not serious and sincere about your commitment, neither will He consider you as one of His own. Jesus came, not just to save people from hell. He wants *so much* more for us. He wants all to have the opportunity to become "one" with Him. He is waiting patiently to bless you in so many ways.

> *Just saying a "sinner's" prayer to gain salvation is not a "Get out of hell free" card.*

Our fruit will confirm our conversion and it will be visible. James tells us in James 2:17, "So also faith by itself, if it does not have works, is dead." He reminds us also in James 1:22-25,

"But be doers of the word, and not hearers only, deceiving yourselves. For if anyone is a hearer of the word and not a doer, he is like a man who looks intently at his natural face in a mirror. For he looks at himself and goes away and at once forgets what he was like. But the one who looks into the perfect law, the law of liberty, and perseveres, being no hearer who forgets but a doer who acts, he will be blessed in his doing."

What makes us acceptable to God is a pattern of obedience to the Word of God that is the product of repentance and genuine faith in Jesus Christ and truly surrendering our life in obedience to His Lordship. True faith will not fail to produce the fruit of good works.

> *Repentance itself is not a work, but works are its predictable fruit.*

Repentance itself is not a work, but works are its predictable fruit. Repentance and faith are inseparably linked in Scripture. Repentance means turning from one's sin, and faith is turning to God. They are like opposite sides of the same coin. That is why we associate both with conversion.

Our works, not *unto* our salvation, but *after* salvation—our fruit—is an expression of our gratitude and dedication to Christ, which results from our gratefulness for what God—through Jesus Christ—has done for us. Some examples of a changed life might be a compelling feeling to love the unlovely and feeling guilty when returning to an old sin, which never before brought any remorse.

# CHAPTER 6

## IT'S TIME FOR A PERSONAL ASSESSMENT

Something else we must not overlook is Jesus not only died for us, but He also conquered death; therefore, when He rose from the dead, He conquered Satan's power. The twentieth chapter of John tells us about His glorious triumph over death. And because of that, He can give eternal life to all who believe in Him. He is the only religious leader of all time who is alive today—whose tomb is empty. All other religious leaders of other (false) religions are still in their grave. "I am the resurrection and the life. Whoever believes in Me, though he die, yet shall he live, and everyone who lives and believes in Me shall never die" (John 11:25-26). We must accept and embrace that as well. Do you believe this?

I have spent all these many pages describing what a Christian is and is not so that you can examine yourself to reveal your heart to see where you are along the spectrum. Just in case you might find yourself among the deceived, I want you to have the opportunity to get things straight with God before we go on.

In 2 Corinthians 13:5, Paul tells us, "Examine yourselves, to see whether you are in the faith. Test yourselves. Or do you not realize this about yourselves, that Jesus Christ is in you?—unless indeed you fail to meet the test!" If you still are not sure, ask yourself these questions:

- Do you find you are hesitant or unwilling to yield to Christ, and what He asks of you?

- Are you put off or annoyed by the commands of Scripture?

- Does it bother you that Christ and His Word are restrictive?

- Do you dislike that you restrain yourself from doing some sins because of pressure put on you?

- Do you do things because of pride or a desire for self-glory?

- Do you do religious activities and go to church because it seems to be the thing to do, and your friends and family expect you to rather than being internally motivated?

- Is your motivation to impress someone or to check off a box—to earn your way?

- Do you love the world or have trouble letting go of the world around you?

First John 2:15 tells us, "Do not love the world or the things in the world. If anyone loves the world, the love of the Father is not in him." If you are not doing these things out of a love for Christ and a desire to grow spiritually and glorify Him with your life, you may have no foundation or some false beliefs.

Is there anything inside you that makes you think you can earn your way to heaven? If you should believe that, I have a thought-provoking question for you. Wouldn't that be a slap in the face of Jesus who died on the cross for you? Why would He have died such a torturous, horrendous, humiliating death in your place, taking the wrath of God on Himself for the punishment of your sin, if you needed to do **anything** to contribute to your salvation? Faith plus *anything* is considered heresy.

Here's something else to think about—if you have ever considered Christianity (which believes Jesus died on the cross in our place for our sins, then rose from the dead conquering death) is *only one of many ways* to get to heaven, then why in the world would God have put Jesus through such an unspeakable death if it wasn't necessary, and there were other ways to get to heaven? As my former pastor, Lon Solomon, used to say, "Not a sermon, just a thought."

Before we move on, let's review and look at Jesus's sacrificial death just a little deeper as to the value of it and its implications. He was unjustly accused and brutally beaten, almost to death. He died the most horrific physical death ever—in our place. He emotionally and spiritually experienced God's wrath for all the sins of humanity for all time—something I don't think we could ever wrap our head around. Remember, He was fully man as well as fully God while He was here, so experienced everything as a human just as we do.

Why did He do it, and what's in it for you? Just in case you didn't fully grasp the magnitude of what happened here, not only did He die in your place. If you accept this gift of love for you, His death results in providing you with the opportunity to avoid the penalty of eternal damnation. We are talking about "forever" here.

That was His plan all along, and that's why He came. He replaced that default destination of hell, with the privilege to live forever in a perfect world where there is no more pain of any kind—physical, emotional, or spiritual. There is no more adversity—nothing negative—only complete peace, joy, goodness, and unconditional love.

Not only that, but for the remainder of your time on earth, He has provided a way for you to experience a personal relationship, a deep connection with Him along with all the benefits that come with that. I just want to be sure you are clear about what you are leaving on the table if you should walk away from this imitation.

So, I now ask you the Evangelism Explosion[1] questions: Knowing all the above, *"If you were to die tonight, would you go to heaven, or is that something you are still working on?"*

**Possible answers:**

- Yes
- No
- Maybe
- Not sure
- I hope so

*God freely offers forgiveness to those who unreservedly repent and come to Him.*

Let's take care of that right now. If your answer is yes, " *Why would God allow you into His heaven?"* Let's make sure you have the right answer.

Jesus told His disciples in John 14:6, "No one comes to the Father except through Me."

Peter in Acts 4:12 told his audience, "There is salvation in no one else, for there is no other name under heaven given among men by which we must be saved."

Because of Jesus Christ's sacrificial death on the cross on our behalf, God freely offers forgiveness to those who unreservedly repent and come to Him. Isn't that amazing!

# CHAPTER 7

## CAN GOD FORGIVE ME?

Before we move on, let's look at your life from a totally different angle just in case this could be your dilemma. Is it possible you feel like you are so deep in sin or your sin is so terrible that God could/would never forgive you?

Do you possibly believe the Creator of the universe cannot handle forgiving anything? Are you aware of all the nasty things that happened to some of those whose lives are described in Scripture, including adultery, lying, and murder that God forgave through repentance?

Remember Peter, who was one of Jesus's closest disciples, denied Him when He was on trial. Yet God did not give up on him. Peter wept when he realized what he had done. He became one of the most powerful and influential preachers of all time, bringing many thousands to Christ while he was alive and is still contributing to the salvation of millions through his written words even today. When Peter wept over his sin, this account reminds us not only of our weakness but also the richness of divine grace.

*His love is "unconditional" and reaches down to the depths of our sinfulness, pursuing us until we respond.*

Paul, who wrote over half of the New Testament, was killing Christians with the blessing of the Jewish religious leaders of his day, honestly thinking he was doing the right thing when the risen Christ appeared and

*He would much rather spend eternity with you than without you, that's why He sent Jesus.*

spoke to him on the road to Damascus (You can find that amazing story in Acts 9). He was on his way to gather as many followers of "The Way" as he could find and bring back to Jerusalem to imprison them. When he realized Jesus truly was the Messiah, he did a complete about-face, and became the most influential preacher/teacher/church planter of his day. The Holy Spirit has used Paul's letters that appear in the New Testament to convert millions even today.

King David, lusted after Bathsheba, committed adultery with her, and then when she got pregnant, he had her husband killed to cover his sin. When he came to his senses and realized how he had dishonored God with his sin, he repented and wrote the most beautiful prayer of repentance (Psalm 51). God not only forgave him but also called him a man after His own heart.

Many other examples like these are in the Bible. Amazingly, this book is completely open and honest about the bad and the ugly, as well as the good that took place in biblical times. There was no holding back. It's hard to imagine after all God has done for us that we might reject Him, and even harder to understand He could love us after all our disobedience and rejection of Him. However, He has an infinite capacity, and His relentless love is entirely different from ours. His love is "unconditional" and reaches down to the depths of our sinfulness, pursuing us until we respond.

Just to be clear, there is nothing God cannot do, and God *wants* you in His family. He already demonstrated His incredible love for you and will forgive anyone with a repentant heart. He would much rather spend eternity with you than without you, that's why He sent Jesus.

One of our chief purposes while living on this earth is to know God intimately, with reverence and reverent familiarity. That begins with what we call the salvation experience, and our relationship grows over time. If you realize you've not accepted Christ as your personal Savior, there's no better time to do that than right now. It's actually very simple. Christ has already done all the work on the cross for you. All you have to do is respond. Have you believed lies about God that have robbed you from experiencing Him?

After all I have told you about Christ, what do you think of Him, and what will you do with Him? Your response to these truths is crucial, because in the day of judgment, as I mentioned previously, there will be no chance to change your mind and embrace the truth. Paul tells us in Philippians 2:10-11 that "at the name of Jesus every knee should bow, in heaven and on earth

*Christ has already done all the work on the cross for you. All you have to do is respond.*

and under the earth, and every tongue confess that Jesus Christ is Lord, to the glory of God the Father."

That means you can either confess Jesus as Lord right now as a Christ-follower or if you don't, you still will come face to face with the Truth and have to declare Him as Lord when you die apart from Him. Whether you want to believe it or not, the truth is—at that point, if you don't know Him, you will see Him *as* He is and will have to acknowledge Him for *Who* He is, and it will be too late to change your mind. You will have missed the chance not just of a lifetime, but for all of eternity.

Here is a rather sobering Scripture to ponder from Matthew 25:31-34, 41, speaking of the end times when Jesus comes again:

When the Son of Man comes in His glory, and all the angels with Him, then He will sit on His glorious throne. Before Him will be gathered all the nations, and He will separate people one from another as a shepherd separates the sheep from the goats. And He will place the sheep on His right, but the goats on the left. Then the King will say to those on His right, 'Come, you who are blessed by My Father, inherit the kingdom prepared for you from the foundation of the world.' ...Then He will say to those on His left, 'Depart from Me, you cursed, into the eternal fire prepared for the devil and his angels.'

Here are a few questions for you to see if you are ready to commit to becoming a Christ-follower:

- Do you believe Jesus Christ is the Son of God?

- Do you believe He died in your place on the cross to free you from guilt and judgment of sin?

- Do you believe He rose from the grave, breaking the power of death and making a way for you to have eternal life in heaven?

If you believe those things, God invites you to come. As a follower of Christ, *I* invite you to come. Why would you not accept Christ's invitation? What reason could be good enough to turn away from Him and the eternal life He offers?

In the words of C. S. Lewis, who used to be an atheist before he met Christ:

All your life an unattainable ecstasy has hovered just beyond the grasp of your consciousness. The day is coming when you will wake to find, beyond all hope, that you have attained it, or else, that it was within your reach and you have lost it forever.[1]

# CHAPTER 8

## JESUS AND HEAVEN
## ARE A PACKAGE DEAL

Jesus and heaven come as a package. You do not get one without the other. To quote the late D.L. Moody, "Why is it so many people want to enjoy heaven when they die but don't want to be heavenly minded while still alive?"[1] Sorry, but you cannot have it both ways. If you think you can "straddle the fence" with one foot in the world (lacking repentance and unwilling to put away the old life) and one foot in the security of heaven, you are mistaken. Jesus tells us in Revelation 3:16 (the last book of the Bible that talks about the end times) that is being what He calls "lukewarm," and He will "spit," or as some translations say, "spew" or "vomit" you out of His mouth.

Do you think you have plenty of time and can decide later? You have no certainty of tomorrow. During the few months it took me to write this book, a friend discovered she had advanced cancer and a brain tumor. She went through the traditional treatments of chemotherapy and radiation and was improving until doctors discovered the chemo had destroyed her kidneys. She died within a couple of weeks from renal failure. We truly never know when our time on this earth is over, and we *must* be prepared. Thankfully, as a Christ-follower, she is now in the

> *Jesus and heaven come as a package. You do not get one without the other.*

arms of Jesus, but her story could have had a very different ending had she not turned her life over to Christ.

*We truly never know when our time on this earth is over, and we must be prepared.*

If you think you are giving up too much on earth in exchange for heaven, you are sorely mistaken. Eternal life and all its benefits begin the moment you accept Jesus's sacrificial death for an exchanged, eternal life with Christ. Eternal life is not just a quantity of time; it's also a quality of life. The benefits of living "in Christ" now, even while still alive far outweigh life without Him.

I have purposely tried to lay out and explain the sacrifices you'll make when you decide to follow Christ, certainly not to discourage you, but because I don't want you to become disillusioned when you may encounter naysayers, opposition, or possibly even persecution. Yes, it is worth it, but until you become deeply committed, seeing God at work in your life, you could get discouraged.

You will learn how to draw strength from God during those times. I want your decision to be deeply rooted in good soil, so you don't make an emotional decision that doesn't last because of worldly pressures. Roots grow deep when the wind is strong. What I desire for all of us are "Deep Roots" that allow us to process the suffering in our lives to make us become like Jesus. If you still are not convinced and need more proof the gospel story is true, the Bible is reliable, or heaven and hell exist, please read some books I listed in my resource section in the back of this book.

If you have been turned off to Christ and Christianity because of some people you know who claim to be Christians yet do not act Christlike—perhaps far from it, realize we all are fallible human beings, and each has our vulnerabilities and weaknesses. Thus, we will all fail God and others

*Roots grow deep when the wind is strong.*

at times. It is inevitable. This failure is what we call sin, and we all succumb to it from time to time. Some of these individuals who come to mind may be deceived themselves and fall under a category I mentioned earlier, thinking they are a Christian when they are not.

Please don't pass judgment on Christ and miss the opportunity to have a personal, intimate, "never-ending" life-changing experience with the Creator of the universe because of someone else's abysmal or "out of alignment" character, attitude, or actions. We must only look to Christ and His character, attitude, and actions. He is our benchmark—no one else.

If you are concerned about what other people may think of you, may I remind you that the only opinion of you that matters is that of Christ? He is the one who determines your destiny of what your eternity experience will be. Regarding your friends you might be concerned about, when push comes to shove, they won't even be thinking about you.

Every year fifty-four million people die. One thing I mentioned earlier, which I know we can agree upon, is we will all die someday and be a part of that statistic. At some point, a loved one will write your obituary and your eulogy, which someone will read at your funeral. What is your destiny, and what will someone say about you? While no one is guaranteed tomorrow, you now have the opportunity to rewrite your legacy. No one can make this decision for you. This has to be your choice, your decision.

*While no one is guaranteed tomorrow, you now have the opportunity to rewrite your legacy.*

The fact that you even picked up this book tells me God is pursuing you. The fact that you have read this far tells me you are seeking Him. If you can believe this, I guarantee, this is a pursuit you will not regret.

*We must only look to Christ and His character, attitude, and actions. He is our benchmark—no one else.*

Here are the necessary steps to make your personal commitment to Christ:

Recognize and admit you're a sinner and you cannot save yourself no matter how "good" you may think you are.

Repent of your sins and ask Him to forgive you.

Acknowledge Jesus Christ is the Son of God, and only He can save you—there is *nothing* you can do to add to your salvation.

Believe His sacrificial, substitutionary death on the cross was an atonement for your sins, and He died on your behalf. Give Him complete control of every area of your life, and ask Him to be your Savior and Lord.

*Eternal life is not just a quantity of time; it's also a quality of life.*

Please don't be concerned about giving up control. It's for your good. Trust me in this. No doubt, it is the best thing you could ever do! You can pray in your own words, but if you need help, you can pray something like this:

*"Heavenly Father, I believe Jesus Christ is Your Son, and He died on the cross to save me from my sin. I believe He rose again to life, and He invites me to live forever with Him in heaven as part of Your family. Because of what Jesus has done, I ask You to forgive me of my sins and give me eternal life. Help me to live in a way that will please and honor You. Amen."*

Congratulations, and welcome to the family of God! You are now a new person! You have just experienced a rebirth! Second Corinthians

5:17 tells us, "Therefore, if anyone is in Christ, he is a new creation. The old has passed away; the new has come."

*When Christ has the first place in your heart, you will experience victory.*

It doesn't say you are an improved version of your old self but a "new" creature with a new nature! Your spiritual DNA is now different since you now have the "seed" of Christ living in you having been "born again" spiritually. This heart change will result in you living fundamentally differently now that you are "in Christ."

We are all a product of our past, but that no longer defines us. I don't know what you found your security in before, but when you find your identity in the One who created you, it changes your whole perspective on life. How awesome is that! In the confidence it gives you, knowing you are loved, valued, and significant, you no longer will experience a need to impress anyone else.

Because of our selfish nature, which will surface from time to time, your flesh will occasionally seek the approval of others. Still, we must remember we are to live out our lives to the audience of only one—Jesus.It is my prayer that you fall in love with Jesus as I have. If you make Him the priority in your life and learn to make Him Lord as well as Savior, you will experience an abundant, empowered life. When Christ has the first place in your heart, you will experience victory.

*When you find your identity in the One who created you, it changes your whole perspective on life.*

# CHAPTER 9

## WHAT HAPPENS WHEN
## CHRIST BECOMES OUR SAVIOR?

When we turn over our lives to Christ, we literally *do* receive Him in that His Spirit, the Holy Spirit, takes up residence in our hearts. Jesus *IS* our life! Romans 8:9 says: "You, however, are not in the flesh but in the Spirit, if indeed the Spirit of God dwells in you. Anyone who does not have the Spirit of Christ does not belong to Him."

Our new identity is now in Christ! We no longer belong to ourselves or anyone else. We are His! Remember my explanation of the Trinity? The Holy Spirit of God now lives inside you!

We all have a natural tendency to bring some baggage into our adult lives. It's not easy to shake behaviors and attitudes that have been modeled to us and been our "norm" while growing up. You may have had great role models and seen Christlike behavior in your home. If so, that is wonderful, but if you have some lingering wounds, remember you do not have to be stuck with them. With God's help, you can break any chains of bondage and pain, and you can now live with a new identity—in Christ!

As I mentioned earlier, at the point of conversion, Jesus transforms our life. We actually go through a metamorphosis, much like a butterfly. However, the green caterpillar morphs alone inside a cocoon while we transform mostly in community. We cannot live out our Christian life in isolation. We are social creatures and need others to encourage us and also to help hold us accountable.

In our transformation, we first experience a "spiritual birth" by which we receive Christ's righteousness in exchange for our sin. Then we start our "spiritual growth" through which we progressively look like Him, taking on the family resemblance since we now have His spiritual seed within us with the new birth. All things are becoming new. We won't reach "spiritual maturity" until we meet Him face to face, but at that time, we will be like Him (1 John 3:2).

*With God's help, you can break any chains of bondage and pain, and you can now live with a new identity—in Christ!*

You may be wondering, "How am I supposed to feel after I have decided to follow Christ?" That's a great question but a difficult one to answer. There are probably about as many answers as there are people because we could factor in so many things. We all come from different backgrounds and experiences, have different personalities, levels of faith, and varying degrees of commitment. God wants us to live by faith as you will learn, and sometimes we have to step out in faith, believing what God tells us even though we at first may not see Him at work.

The feelings, revelations, and experiences will follow. You may feel like an incredible burden has been lifted, and you may sense an immediate change in your spirit. Or, you may not feel anything at all for a while. That does not mean nothing happened. This is where you must exercise faith while you act on what you know is true, and you will see change over time.

Don't think for a minute you will no longer have problems. You may even have more as you learn how to make this transition. Your new faith will not eliminate your problems but will keep you in a trusting relationship with God in the midst of your difficulties, and He will give you the strength, wisdom, and power to get through them. Your faith has to do with the relationship with your Creator, not your circumstances. Faith is believing what God has said to the point of acting on it whether we feel like it or not.

As we grow in this new life, it's okay to take baby steps. You know how it is when a toddler is learning how to walk. They take a few steps, and they fall. Do you scold them for falling? No, you encourage them to get up and try again to see if they will go farther the next time. They keep trying and falling until finally, they get it. God is the same way with us as we struggle to learn this new way of life. He is our biggest supporter and cheerleader all the way. We need to be sure we are teachable, as we step out—reach out to Him for guidance, and follow His lead.

> *Faith is believing what God has said to the point of acting on it whether we feel like it or not.*

It is essential during this process to stop trying so hard, and allow Jesus to live His life through you in the power of the Holy Spirit so that your behavior and lifestyle matches what is true. Try as you might, you can never perfectly or completely imitate Christ. You will end up discouraged with failure time and time again. Just rest in Him and let Him do the work.

Paul, in Galatians 2:20, says of himself after his conversion: "I have been crucified with Christ. It is no longer I who live, but Christ who lives in me. And the life I now live in the flesh I live by faith in the Son of God, who loved me and gave Himself for me." This is true for any of us who have given our heart to Jesus.

The only thing is, this liberating Spirit only applies to the places where we relinquish control. If you are holding onto an area in your life and don't want to let go, you will not experience the true freedom and victory in your life. That only comes with complete and total surrender.

## IS THERE ANY CHANCE
## I COULD LOSE MY SALVATION?

You may be wondering if you can ever lose your salvation. That's an honest question. I became a Christian at a very young age, but was brought up in a denomination that did not teach about assurance of salvation or "eternal security." I thought I needed to ask Jesus into my heart continually, so to be sure I was covered, I would sing the song, "Lord, I Want to be a Christian in My Heart," every night when I went to bed. (Kind of like saying the prayer, "Now I lay me down to sleep.")

When I was a sophomore in high school, I visited my uncle's church, and the Sunday school teacher asked me if I had ever asked Jesus into my heart. I told her, "Oh, I do that every night."

She said, "Honey, you don't have to do that! You only have to ask Him once. He will never leave you!"

Wow, was that ever good news! That is what I want to tell you today. Once you have sincerely turned your life over to Christ, He will never leave you nor forsake you (Hebrews 13:5). John 10:27-28 tells us, "My sheep hear My voice, and I know them, and they follow Me. I give them eternal life, and they will never perish, and no one will snatch them out of My hand."

One wonderful fact regarding our salvation in Christ is that it is irreversible; it cannot be undone. Once we are truly saved, we are saved forever because our salvation has at its basis the very nature and person of God Himself. Jesus tells us in John 15:16: "You did not choose me, but I chose you."

Salvation was God's idea, not ours. He pursued each of us until we responded. I have never quite gotten over the cross, the sacrifice that took place there, and the fact Jesus "chose" me. He chose you as well! Can you believe that? What a fantastic gift.

# CHAPTER 10

## WHAT SHOULD YOU EXPECT NOW?

When we are born of God, we get His nature, but He does not immediately take away all the old nature. Each species of animal and bird is true to its nature. You can tell the nature of the dove or canary bird. The horse is true to his nature, the cow is true to hers. But a man has two natures, and do not let the world or Satan make you think the old nature is extinct, because it is not.

Though it is subdued, the old nature in the believer never dies; and unless you are watchful and prayerful, it will gain the upper hand, and rush you into sin. Someone has pointed out that 'I' is the center of S-I-N. It is the medium through which Satan acts. And so the worst enemy you have to overcome after all is yourself.[1]

I know because I have been there. I can speak from experience it can be quite a struggle, especially when, in our residual sinful nature, we take back control at times. That's the problem with being a "living" sacrifice. It means we'll get up on the altar of surrender, but then we keep crawling down when times get tough. ☺

I used to wonder and often would ask God why He didn't take away my sin nature when I became a believer. He revealed to me that if there was not that internal struggle to turn to Him for guidance and direction, I would end up considering myself to be rather self-sufficient and would feel no need to depend on Him. He wants us to rest in Him. He wants to give us His best—His wisdom, power, peace, and joy—all things, but He cannot do that if we are pushing through life in our strength.

The Holy Spirit, which comes to live inside us when we become a follower of Christ, is much better at leading and guiding our lives than we ever could. Still, sometimes we forget that and take back control, to our detriment.

Once you become a Christ-follower, your life mission is to glorify God in and through your life. Once you have truly made this commitment, your life will be transformed, and you will desire to do this. In Romans 12:2, Paul tells us: "Do not be conformed to this world, but be transformed by the renewal of your mind, that by testing you may discern what is the will of God, what is good and acceptable and perfect."

Over time as your life transforms more and more in the image of Christ. Your life and countenance will radiate with the love of Jesus, and you will draw others to Him.

Christ is invisible, but now He lives in and through you; and you are to be an extension of Him to the world, exemplifying His life of unconditional love, humility, grace, and servanthood, and to live out His character qualities—the fruit of the Spirit. Galatians 5:22–24 states: "But the fruit of the Spirit is love, joy, peace, patience, kindness, goodness, faithfulness, gentleness, self-control; against such things there is no law. And those who belong to Christ Jesus have crucified the flesh with its passions and desires."

When I became serious about my faith as a college student, I found these verses and clung to them to be my life's goal, with God's help—to achieve these character qualities in my life—a goal that has served me well all these years.

There was never a man who walked with more integrity than Jesus. In fact, He is the epitome of integrity we should emulate. This is the kind of change you can see taking place in your life. Don't be discouraged if you feel so far from achieving this. Remember, life is a journey.

No doubt about it, the Christian life is hard work. Christianity involves systematically striving to implement the truths of God's Word into our lives. Don't worry. There's no way we could ever do any of this on our own. But as a Christ-follower, you have the power of the Holy Spirit in your life, which gives you the ability to do all things within the will of God. If we walk by the Spirit, then we "will not gratify the desires of the flesh" (Galatians 5:16). Over time, you will learn how to "rest" in Him.

# CHAPTER 11

## NEXT STEPS

You will now want to grow in your knowledge of Christ and your obedience to Him. God gave you everything you need to overcome any struggle with the help of the Holy Spirit, which now lives in you. What is God's plan for you? He wants you to trust Him. How do you trust someone you don't know? How do you get to know God? By prayer and studying His Word. It's through these activities that He speaks and reveals Himself to us.

Our generation lacks a sense of wonder and reverence for God. There is a tendency to want to bring Him down to our level. While we have direct access to Him as a Christ-follower, that privilege was bought with the price of the death of His Son. As you meditate on that thought, it should cause you to treasure your time with Him in prayer and study of His Word, and you will come to realize what a blessing it is.

You should not consider prayer as a discipline or duty, but a delight. Worship will become an activity you will grow to love and seize with heartfelt gratitude. You will learn praise is a powerful weapon in the heart of a believer and will ambush the enemy every time he tries to discourage, cause doubt or fear, or turn your priorities and affections away from God.

**Read the Bible.** This is how you hear from God to learn how to live a life that honors Him and gives testimony to others that Jesus has made a difference in your life. It is how you come to know the heart of God and is the best self-improvement course ever devised. "Your Word is a lamp to my feet and a light to my path" (Psalm 119:105).

If you are unfamiliar with the Bible, I recommend you start with the New Testament to learn the life and teachings of Jesus and His followers. I would recommend getting *John MacArthur's Study Bible* or the *ESV Study Bible*. Both have very comprehensive study notes to explain some Scriptures that might be a bit confusing. I recommend the English Standard Version (ESV).

Over time, learn how to meditate on the Word. That means simply to camp out on a verse or passage and ask God to reveal the truths about Himself until it becomes real and personal to you. That way, the truth moves from your head to your heart, which will result in obedience. That's where you want to end up. It's kind of hard to obey what you don't know, so reading the Bible is vital for your growth. Let the Word do the work in your heart.

*Let the Word do the work in your heart.*

As you read the Scriptures, ask yourself these three questions: What does it say? What does it mean? What does it mean to me? Each time we read the Bible, we must prepare ourselves to obey what we are told to do.

Many key verses can help you through difficult times—promises of God that can be so healing and meaningful. I have included a short list of some of my favorites in the resources section in the back of this book. I encourage you not only to meditate on these but also to memorize them. There will be times when you will recall these, and they will bring much comfort to you.

When you allow His truth to touch you in the deepest corner of your soul, the Holy Spirit will transform you into the image of Christ. If you have tried to read the Bible before and didn't understand it, that's because

72

without the Holy Spirit indwelling you to interpret the Scriptures for you, most often they will not make much sense. Having the mind of Christ, with the benefit of His Spirit, you will gain supernatural wisdom, knowledge, and understanding, and you will find yourself falling in love with the Word of God. In fact, once you start tasting the words of God, you will develop an insatiable appetite for it.

**Pray.** God wants men and women who will come before Him with genuine needs and pray, believing He will answer. If you have prayed before but felt like your prayers have not gone any higher than the ceiling, then that is because until we become a child of God, He usually only responds to prayers of repentance as we honestly seek to know Him and the truth of His Word.

We must develop the discipline to daily block off time to meet with God—our Creator, Savior, and Lord—to get honest and real with Him. I find first thing in the morning works best for me in that it gets my heart right from the outset. This time of prayer is not a chore but a privilege I look forward to every day.

As a Christ-follower, we are called to humility, and the quality of our prayer life is the barometer of our humility. By communicating regularly with God through prayer, you will keep your focus on eternal things. Your desire should be to bring God glory through your life. Paul instructs us in Philippians 4:6-7, "Do not be anxious about anything, but in everything by prayer and supplication with thanksgiving let your requests be made known to God. And the peace of God, which surpasses all understanding, will guard your hearts and your minds in Christ Jesus."

> *The quality of our prayer life is the barometer of our humility.*

I recommend praying this way: **ACTS.** This is an acronym for **Adoration, Confession, Thanksgiving, and Supplication.**

**Adoration:** Start by praising God for His many attributes and whatever comes to mind for which to worship Him (showing adoration). A list of many of His attributes is in the appendix. If you have trouble coming up with what to say, look at Psalm 103 and recite that for starters. We need to be sure we see God for who He is and be devoted to honoring Him. Praise is rooted not in our circumstances, but in the nature and trustworthiness of God. Someone has said (paraphrasing), "If we have a small God, we have big problems, but if we have a big God, we have small problems." There is a lot of truth to that. How big is God to you right now?

**Confession:** Then, spend some time asking God to show you what you need to confess to become clean before Him. Ask Him to search your heart. Confession is agreeing with God about your sin, whereas your natural inclination may be to justify it rather than admit it for what it is. This requires honesty. Psalm 145:18 says, "The LORD is near to all who call on Him, to all who call on Him in truth." God gives us a promise in 1 John 1:9, where He tells us, "If we confess our sins, He is faithful and just to forgive us our sins and to cleanse us from all unrighteousness."

God will be specific as He points out areas of your life that you need to confess. That is called conviction. If you are feeling condemnation, and have vague thoughts of being no good or not enough, etc., that is from the enemy and not from God who lovingly points our particular sins that you need to address.

You cannot have Scripture fill your heart and continue to habitually sin against God. An incredible example of repentance before God is in beautiful Psalm 51 written by King David, who had sinned mightily, but because of his repentant heart, God restored the joy of his salvation and ended up calling him a man after His own heart.

74

**Thanksgiving:** Next, spend some time thanking God for your many blessings. As a Christ-follower, we have so much for which to be grateful. When we focus on thanking God, it takes our focus off ourselves and on who God is. We are to thank Him *for* everything and *in* everything. Paul tells us in 1 Thessalonians 5:16–18, "Rejoice always, pray without ceasing, give thanks in all circumstances; for this is the will of God in Christ Jesus for you." This implies we choose as an act of our will to thank God for the good, the difficult, and even the unknown because He is faithful, sovereign, and in control. If you need help to get started, try reading Psalm 100:1–5.

**Supplication:** Supplication just means to lay your requests before Him, praying for yourself and asking things for others. Be specific, God-honoring, and with the intent of praying in line with His will in all things. Jesus promised: "If you abide in Me, and My words abide in you, ask whatever you wish, and it will be done for you" (John 15:7).

**Seek Christian fellowship.** Meeting regularly with Christian brothers and sisters allows you to follow Jesus's example of love and to fulfill His command to "love one another: just as I have loved you" (John 13:34). Seek out mature Christians who can encourage and challenge you in your new-found faith. Having an accountability partner (someone you can trust, can be honest with and will hold you responsible and accountable to live your new life appropriately) can be priceless. Who you hang out with is important.

*Who you hang out with is important.*

**Find a Bible-believing/teaching church.** Just as Jesus surrounded Himself daily with His disciples and followers, you need to find a place where you can meet with other Christians. There you will find joy and encouragement in the fellowship of God's people. "And let us consider how to stir up one another to love and good works, not neglecting to meet

*Baptism does not save you but is an outward expression and testimony of the inward change that has taken place in your heart.*

together, as is the habit of some, but encouraging one another" (Hebrews 10:24–25).

**Get baptized.** This is something you need to do because it is a command from Jesus. Baptism is a way to make a public profession of your faith that you have put your trust in Jesus for your salvation. The act of baptism does not save you but is an outward expression and testimony of the inward change that has taken place in your heart. It is the first thing Jesus did, even before He started His ministry. He was baptized by John the Baptist. "And he commanded them to be baptized in the name of Jesus Christ" (Acts 10:48).

It is my prayer God will transform your heart through the gospel of Jesus Christ by the in-depth and continuous work of the Holy Spirit as you make Jesus the object of your affections. Transformation does not come from knowledge but from *obedience* to what we know. It doesn't come out of trying hard, but by believing the truth.

Now that you have a relationship with God, that places infinite value on your life. The treasure of God's wisdom and knowledge is now available to you through Christ as well as His perfect love. You now have access to peace that passes all understanding as well as a supernatural compassion for others. When Jesus lives in you, everything available to Him also dwells in you.

*Transformation does not come from knowledge but from obedience to what we know.*

Remember, the same God who created the universe, the same Jesus who rose from the dead, and the same Holy Spirit who inspired the writing of the Holy Scriptures (the Bible), which is the book we live by, actually lives in you! You have direct access to God and His wisdom. How tremendous is that!

One heart change you should notice in yourself, especially if it is contrary to how you used to be, is an attitude of gratitude. When you are a follower of Christ, there is no reason *not* to be grateful, no matter what the circumstances, and that does not come naturally. We have *so* much for which to be thankful. Did you know your brain cannot be disgruntled and grateful at the same time? So, you have to choose what kind of attitude you will have each day—moment by moment.

When we have Jesus, we not only have eternal life; we also have so much more. *He* is *all* we need. He is sovereign, in control, has our back, and always has our best interests at heart. He is faithful to do all that He promised.

Life is full of choices, and I think you will find yourself making much better choices now! When we live in light of eternity, our values change, don't they? I am so excited for you and for what God has in store for you in your new life! Jesus will give you everything you need to live for Him. Now you also have been given an incredible new "life's purpose."

> *Jesus will give you everything you need to live for Him.*

At some point, we all ask ourselves three questions:

- Who am I? (Identity)
- Where do I belong? (Security)
- What am I supposed to do? (Significance)

First, you need to realize you are fearfully and wonderfully made by the Creator of the universe. Your identity is now in Christ. Besides creating the entire universe and all its galaxies, He created you and me—

77

in His image to be in a relationship with Him and for a specific purpose. You are special in His eyes. You belong to Him, and you contain specific qualities unique to you—and God does not make mistakes. It's never too early, but most people don't get around to asking about the purpose for their life until they start going through a midlife crisis. It *is* a crisis to believe the life left behind has been pretty much one where the focus has been primarily living for oneself.

For help to figure out your life's purpose going forward, and now that you know where you will spend eternity, be sure to read my book, *Living the Life You Always Wanted—Experience Peace, Joy, Power, and Perfect Love in Times of Uncertainty.* This book will teach you how to experience an empowered life. Let's see how you can make the most of what you have learned so far, and experience an amazingly abundant life fulfilling God's purpose for you, making the most out of the days you have left on this earth!

Your first step should be to "Pay it forward" and share this book with those you know who could benefit from its content. This book contains information you do not want to keep to yourself! Actually, before giving it away, I would recommend reading it again. Now that you are a Christ-follower, many Scriptures I quoted that may not have made sense initially, probably will now that you have the Holy Spirit to help interpret them. He will open your eyes to the truth so that you can see things from God's perspective. Read them slowly and ponder them, asking the Spirit to help you understand them. It will be a great review for you as well.

## PERSONAL REFLECTION AND CALL TO ACTION:

Going forward: What do you need to say, "No" to? What do you need to say, "Yes" to?

Who will you call or text today to tell of the life-changing decision you just made and to help hold you accountable for this?

If you think this book would benefit others, would you be willing to go to Amazon and leave a review? It would mean so much and who knows, your review might influence someone to read this and take that step of faith and become a follower of Christ. How exciting it would be to share in that!

Scanning this QR code will take you to your review page after signing in:

It would mean so much to me if you would let me know if the message of this book changed your life in any way. Did you pray to receive Christ as your personal Savior? Did you share it with someone who did? I would love to know that. If you prayed a prayer repenting of your sins and have turned your life over to Christ, would you shoot me an email to let me know? I would be so honored if you would send an email to NewBeliever@debbysibert.com so I can pray for you. Your message will come directly to me, and I would be blessed to pray for you as you begin your new journey with Christ.

Be sure to check out my website: http://www.DebbySibert.com to get the latest information about all and my newest publications. There you also will find a contact form if you have any questions or concerns. In the "Author" section you can see the topics on which I am available to speak for women's groups at your church or para-church organization. If you follow "Debby Sibert Author" on Facebook, you will receive my daily inspirational quotes.

God bless you on your journey,

Debby Sibert

# Do You Want Debby's *FREE* Follow-Up Book?

Debby always has a booklet available to help her readers along in their spiritual journey. These giveaways complement each of her books. The companion booklet for this book, a 41 page .pdf is a perfect follow-up from this book. It is titled, *How to Live Your New Life in Christ.* It's a study of the "Fruit of the Spirit" discussed briefly in this book as well as other character traits of Christ that we need to learn how to emulate.

If you recall, she said studying these character qualities became her life's goal and benchmark for how to live a Christ-like life. If you'd like to receive this eBook for free, and to be notified when she's launching any new free or paid books please consider signing up at the following link. In fact those who sign up will be the first to be notified when new books are available for purchase as well.

Whenever she launces a book, it is highly discounted at launch. Check out the current free book and download it for free here: https://tinyurl.com/GrowNextSteps or use this **QR** code to access sign up form.

If you like audio books and are *not yet a member of "Audible"* you can get this audio book (*Where Will You Spend Eternity?*) for free by signing up at the following link.

# APPENDIX
## ATTRIBUTES OF GOD

This list is not exhaustive, but contains plenty of God's attributes to blow the human mind about God's unfathomable character. I could quote dozens of verses to back up each attribute of God listed here, but I picked one for each to help if you would like to expand your knowledge and understanding of each.

**Accessible** – He lives in every believer, and we can access Him at any time. (Galatians 2:20)

**Compassionate** – The outpouring of Christ's blood to make grace available to all of us reflects God's compassionate heart. (Psalm 103:13)

**Creator** – No one Created God. There never was a time when He did not exist. Only He can bring something out of nothing, and He created everything. The same God who created the entire universe and all its galaxies created, loves, and knows you by name! He created us all for a special purpose. (Genesis 1)

**Eternal** – He always was and always will be. He exists outside the boundary of space and time. Because He is eternal, He offers us eternal life with Him, which He alone can give. (Romans 1:20)

**Faithful** – We can always trust Him in all things and to keep His promises. This is the basis of our confidence in Him. He can never *not* be faithful as that is part of His divine nature and would require Him to change. He cannot cease to be who He is. (Deuteronomy 7:9)

**Father** – He is Father only to those who believe in His Son, Jesus Christ. We are all His creation, but we are only His children if we are willing to call Him Father. He lovingly protects, cares for, and disciplines His children. Hi longs for an intimate relationship with us. (John 14:23)

**Forgiving** – Forgiveness is an outpouring of God's love. None deserve it, yet God offers it freely to all who accept the substitutionary, sacrificial death of Jesus Christ on the cross. (1 John 1:9)

**Glorious** – God's glory exhibits the total of all His many attributes. He is infinitely beautiful and magnificent, full of grace and mercy. The Lord Jesus reveals God's glory completely. His radiance and beauty emanate from all that He is and does. Our whole existence and purpose are to glorify and bring glory to Him. (Psalm 19:1)

**Good** – He is infinitely, unchangingly kind, and full of hope and goodwill. We see God's goodness in His love and faithfulness. Even when bad things happen, God always promises to make all things work together for good. (Romans 8:28)

**Gracious** – Grace is God's kindness and favor to all of us who do not deserve it. He is slow to anger and great in lovingkindness. Grace is so much a part of God and so inextinguishable that He can no more hide it than the sun can hide its brightness. (Ephesians 2:8–9)

**Guide** – God is our light, illuming our path, guidance us in the way we should go. Without His direction, we would stumble and fall like those probing their way in the darkness. (Proverbs 3:5–6)

**Healer** – God is the great Physician and has the power to heal at will, miraculously, or through traditional methods. (Psalm 103:1–3)

**Holy** – God is high and lifted up and set apart above His creation. He is always perfect with a purity that is incapable of being anything other than what it is. Holy is the way God is, and He is the standard. He has set us apart to be holy as He is holy. Because He is holy, all His attributes are holy. (Isaiah 6:3)

**Immutable** – God and nothing about Him will ever change. He cannot change. While it is impossible for man *not* to change, it is impossible for God *to* change. He will never be more or less holy than He is right now. Because He never changes, we can always trust Him and His promises. (Hebrews 13:8)

**Impartial** – It does not matter your status, race, or reputation. God saves people regardless of what they have done or will do. God will always do right by every person in every situation. (Romans 2:11)

**Incomprehensible** – We will never be able to understand God's thoughts and ways, which are much higher than ours. Because of His Word and His indwelling Spirit, we can understand all we need to know. (Isaiah 55:8–9)

**Infinite** – God is self-existing, without origin. He is Eternal with no beginning and no end. He always existed and always will. God's love and power have no limits. God, the Father, Son, and Spirit are all the same: infinite. (Revelation 22:13)

**Invisible** – Since God is a spirit, we cannot see Him. However, God has made Himself visible through the person of Jesus Christ. We can experience Jesus's presence through the Holy Spirit with us now, and when He returns, we will see Him as He is, face to face. (Colossians 1:15)

**Jealous** – God's jealousy is far different than human jealousy. His is one of protective love. He is righteously angry when His children choose to devote their time and attention to lesser things. Out of His love for us, when we turn our back on Him, He pursues us with all that He has. (Exodus 34:14)

**Joy** – Just like God is love and truth, He also is joy. Our joy is rooted in who God is. We can experience internal joy no matter what our circumstances because God reigns. (Nehemiah 8:10)

**Just** – God's justice is unchangeably right and perfect. His decisions are always a reflection of His righteous character. Because He is holy, He cannot ignore sin. But, because He is just, God will never punish His children, who have put their trust in Him, accepting the sacrifice Jesus paid on the cross for our sins. (1 Corinthians 6:11)

**Love** – God has always been love. It's who He is. It is an essential attribute of God. If He stopped *loving*, He would have to stop *being*. His love never fails. The love of God is eternal, sovereign, unchanging, and infinite. God loves the world, and when we receive His Son as our Savior, then we have the capacity to love God and others with that save love. (1 John 4:16)

**Merciful** – Miraculously, God in His mercy does not give us what our sins deserve. He is unchangeably compassionate and kind. He forgives and restores those who humbly repent and turn to Him in believing faith. His mercies are new every morning. (Ephesians 2:4–5)

**Omnipotent (all-powerful)** – God has unlimited power, authority, and influence overall. He does all that He wills to do with no limits. Nothing can stop God or stand in the way of Him accomplishing His will. (Jeremiah 32:17)

**Omnipresent (everywhere)** – God is everywhere. There's nowhere in the universe where God is not present. There is no way to hide from God. Satan has restrictions and can only be in one place at a time, but God has the power to always be everywhere at all times. (Psalm 139)

**Omniscient (all-knowing)** – Nothing ever surprises God. He knows all there is to know. He possesses perfect knowledge and has no need to learn. He knows all our thoughts, words, and deeds. Only God knows all things, and we can trust Him to judge perfectly. (Psalm 147:5)

**Patient** – God is patient – an attribute we would do well to learn. He could put an end to human rebellion immediately, but He loves His creation and does not wish for anyone to perish, so He allows time for repentance. He is slow to anger, but one day God will come to judge all people. (2 Peter 3:9)

**Perfect** – God is perfect and upright in everything He does and says. All His attributes, His revelation, His works, and His Judgments, are entirely free of fault or defect of any kind. Everything He is, does, or says is flawless and true, including His Word—the Scriptures. (Psalm 18:30)

**Person** – God is an actual person, not an idea or an impersonal force. We were made in His image, so like us, He has identity and personality. He is one being in three Persons, God, Son, and Holy Spirit, equal in essence, but each with their own function. All work together to accomplish our salvation. (John 5:26)

**Preserver** – When we become a Christ-follower, we can be assured that He will complete the work He began in us. There is nothing we can do to lose our salvation. He preserves us so that He can accomplish His will and purpose for us. (Philippians 1:6)

**Provider** – God provides whatever we need. He provides for our daily needs, as well as a way out of temptation, and protects us from evil. He is the great I AM, meaning He is ALL we could ever need. God's greatest gift to us is His Son. Because of that, we can trust Him to give us everything else we need. (1 Corinthians 10:13)

**Righteous** – We can count on God to be right in all He does. All His words, actions, and plans are always pure and right. God Has no sin, is perfect in every way, and certainly never lies. We can count on Him to be fair, just, and faithful in all He does. Because God is righteous, He expects us to be righteous as well. Even the best person cannot be perfectly righteous, but God sees His children through the blood of Christ that was shed for us and therefore clothed with the righteousness of Christ. (Isaiah 41:10)

**Savior** – Thankfully, God reaches down and rescue sinners from the penalty of death and hell that we deserve. Because we are dead in our sin, we have no power to save ourselves. God's plan from the beginning was to save His children from the penalty, power, and presence of sin. He sent Jesus to live the perfect life we could not live, and He died in our place for our sin, exchanging His life for ours. On the cross, Jesus paid the ransom for us, which satisfied God's wrath against our sin. That leaves no punishment for us, His children. Jesus saved His children from sin's power and gives us new desires and a unique ability to fight sin through the power of the Holy Spirit which indwells the heart of every believer at conversion. (2 Corinthians 5:21)

**Self-sufficient** – God has no needs. Because of this, we can go to Him to satisfy all our needs. He can do immeasurably more than all we ask or imagine according to His power at work in us. (Romans 11:33–36)

**Sovereign** – God controls all things, at all times, and there's nothing outside of His control. What God plans happens. Nothing happens out of His authority, and not even Satan can stop or change God's plans. He is free to do whatever He wants. When God permits evil, we can trust that in His faithfulness and sovereignty, He has planned to use it for our good and for His glory. No one can keep God from accomplishing His plan because He alone has the power to do it. (Luke 1:37)

**Transcendent** – God is exalted far above the created universe, so far above, that human thought cannot even imagine it. We should be in total awe of Him. (Psalm 97:9)

**Wise** – God is not only all-knowing. But also He is full of perfect, unchanging wisdom. He always uses His knowledge to do exactly what is right. The idea that God is infinitely wise is at the root of all truth. God's Word is full of His wisdom. All wisdom comes from God. As a Christ-follower, we have access to the wisdom of God. How amazing is that! If we are to be truly wise, we must seek Him. (James 3:17)

# Promises of God to Help You on Your Journey

These are some of my favorite verses to help me whenever I am struggling in specific areas of my life. I know they are true because they are from God. He is always faithful and completely trustworthy to carry out His promises. These verses should help you find peace, comfort, and strength as well as sustain you when you feel discouraged or distant from God.

**When you are tired and weary:**

"Come to Me, all who labor and are heavy laden, and I will give you rest. Take My yoke upon you, and learn from Me, for I am gentle and lowly in heart, and you will find rest for your souls. For My yoke is easy, and My burden is light." – Matthew 11:28–30

"But they who wait for the LORD shall renew their strength; they shall mount up with wings like eagles; they shall run and not be weary; they shall walk and not faint." – Isaiah 40:31

**When things seem impossible:**

"Jesus looked at them and said, 'With man it is impossible, but not with God. For all things are possible with God.'"– Mark 10:27

"All things are possible for one who believes." – Mark 9:23

"I can do all things through Him who strengthens me." – Philippians 4:13

"And my God will supply every need of yours according to His riches in glory in Christ Jesus." – Philippians 4:19

**When struggling in your faith:**

"Therefore I tell you, whatever you ask in prayer, believe that you have received it, and it will be yours." – Mark 11:24

"What then shall we say to these things? If God is for us, who can be against us?" – Romans 8:31

**When needing guidance and wisdom:**

"If any of you lacks wisdom, let him ask God, who gives generously to all without reproach, and it will be given him." – James 1:5

"Trust in the LORD with all your heart, and do not lean on your own understanding. In all your ways acknowledge Him, and He will make straight your paths." – Proverbs 3:5-6

**When feeling unworthy:**

"Look at the birds of the air: they neither sow nor reap nor gather into barns, and yet your heavenly Father feeds them. Are you not of more value than they?" – Matthew 6:26

"But even the hairs of your head are all numbered. Fear not, therefore; you are of more value than many sparrows." – Matthew 10: 30–31

**When feeling fearful:**

"Be strong and courageous. Do not be frightened, and do not be dismayed, for the LORD your God is with you wherever you go." – Joshua 1:9

"Fear not, for I am with you; be not dismayed, for I am your God; I will strengthen you, I will help you, I will uphold you with My righteous right hand." – Isaiah 41:10

"For God gave us a spirit not of fear but of power and love and self-control." – 2 Timothy 1:7

"The LORD is my light and my salvation; whom shall I fear? The LORD is the stronghold of my life; of whom shall I be afraid?" – Psalm 27:1

**When discouraged:**

"For I know the plans I have for you, declares the LORD, plans for welfare and not for evil, to give you a future and a hope." – Jeremiah 29:11

"And we know that for those who love God all things work together for good, for those who are called according to His purpose." – Romans 8:28

"I have said these things to you, that in Me you may have peace. In the world you will have tribulation. But take heart; I have overcome the world." – John 16:33

"Let us then with confidence draw near to the throne of grace, that we may receive mercy and find grace to help in time of need." – Hebrews 4:16

**When feeling far from God:**

"'For the mountains may depart and the hills be removed, but My steadfast love shall not depart from you, and My covenant of peace shall not be removed,' says the LORD, who has compassion on you."– Isaiah 54:10

"Delight yourself in the LORD, and He will give you the desires of your heart." – Psalm 37:4

"Do not be anxious about anything, but in everything by prayer and supplication with thanksgiving let your requests be made known to God."– Philippians 4:6

"For I am sure that neither death nor life, nor angels nor rulers, nor things present nor things to come, nor powers, nor height nor depth, nor anything else in all creation, will be able to separate us from the love of God in Christ Jesus our Lord."– Romans 8:38–39

**When you feel defeated:**

"Submit yourselves therefore to God. Resist the devil, and he will flee from you." – James 4:7

"If we confess our sins, He is faithful and just to forgive us our sins and to cleanse us from all unrighteousness." – 1 John 1:9

"He who is in you is greater than he who is in the world."– 1 John 4:4

"Take My yoke upon you, and learn from Me, for I am gentle and lowly in heart, and you will find rest for your souls. For My yoke is easy and My burden is light." – Matthew 11:29-30

"Casting all your anxieties on Him, because He cares for you." – 1 Peter 5:7

"Even though I walk through the valley of the shadow of death, I will fear no evil, for You are with me; Your rod and Your staff, they comfort me." – Psalm 23:4

**Remembering to keep the main thing the main thing:**

"But seek first the kingdom of God and His righteousness, and all these things will be added to you." – Matthew 6:33

"Commit your work to the Lord, and your plans will be established." – Proverbs 16:3

# Resources

*Living the Life You Always Wanted*
   Experience Peace, Joy, Power, and Perfect Love in Uncertain Times – Debby Sibert

*Forever is a Long Time to be Wrong* – Debby Sibert

*Your Antidote for Depression, Anxiety, or Fear*
   Learn How to Experience Peace and Joy During Adversity and Uncertain Times – Debby Sibert

*Case for Christ, Case for Faith, Case for Easter* – Lee Strobel

*Evangelism Explosion* – D. James Kennedy

*Evidence that Demands a Verdict* – Josh McDowell

*Experiencing God* – Henry Blackaby

*Follow Me* – David Platt

*Heaven* – Randy Acorn

*More than a Carpenter* – Josh McDowell

*Radically Obedient, Radically Blessed* – Lysa TerKeurst

*Rewire Your Heart* – David Bowden

*So You Want to be Like Christ?* – Charles Swindoll

*The Real Heaven* – Chip Ingram

*What Every Christian Ought to Know* – Adrian Roger

# NOTES:

**Introduction**

1   Randy Alcorn. "Can You Know You're Going to Heaven?" Eternal Perspective Ministries, March 5, 2010. https://www.epm.org/resources/2010/Mar/5/can-you-know-youre-going-heaven/.

**Chapter 1**

1. Frank Newport. "Most Americans Still Believe in God." Gallup, June 29, 2016. https://news.gallup.com/poll/193271/americans-believe-god.aspx

2. K Connie Kang. "Most Believe in Heaven and Think They'll go There." Deseret News. October 25, 2013. https://www.deseret.com/2003/10/25/19792181/most-believe-in-heaven-and-think-they-ll-go-there.

**Chapter 2**

1. "Christian." https://www.dictionary.com/browse/christian?s=t Accessed May 3, 2020.

2. Butler, Trent C. Editor. Entry for "Christian." Holman Bible Dictionary. https://www.studylight.org/dictionaries/hbd/c/christian.html. 1991.

**Chapter 3**

1. "Sin."https://www.dictionary.com/browse/sin?s=t   Accessed May 3, 2020.

1. Butler, Trent C. Editor. Entry for "Sin." Holman Bible Dictionary. https://www.studylight.org/dictionaries/hbd/s/sin.html. 1991.

2. David Bowden, *Rewire Your Heart*. (Nashville: Thomas Nelson, 2018) xi–xii, 3.

**Chapter 6**

1. D. James Kennedy, *Evangelism Explosion*. (Wheaton: Tyndale House, 1983) 17–18.

**Chapter 7**

1. C. S. Lewis, *The Problem of Pain*. (London: The Centenary Press, 1940) 131.

**Chapter 8**

1. D.L. Moody, *Heaven* (Chicago: The Moody Press 1900)

**Chapter 10**

1. D. L. Moody, *The Overcoming Life and Other Sermons*. (Chicago: Bible Institute Colportage Association, 1896) 15–16.

# OTHER BOOKS BY DEBBY SIBERT

## *God's Antidote for Depression, Anxiety, or Fear*
### *Learn How to Experience Peace and Joy During Difficult and Uncertain Times*

Do you ever wonder, "Where is God" when going through challenging times? Does He seem distant, or even non-existent? What is the biggest crisis you are experiencing right now?

We are currently living in extraordinary times, causing much anxiety even for the strongest temperament. There are many reasons individuals experience fear, anxiety, and even depression, and our world seems to be growing more and more fearful every day. If we ever lived in an uncertain time with an unclear future and reason to fear it is now.

Fear is a natural response for humans and has its place to help keep us safe. However, living in fear is counter-productive and is not an option if we are going to get through any difficult circumstances. We cannot allow ourselves to get stuck there and dwell on these negative issues.

Believe it or not, there is a way to experience peace in the midst of all of this and that is what I will be unpacking in this book. We have many choices in life. Every day we're making more choices than we realize. Peace is another choice that we can make over fear and anxiety. It takes recognizing where our mind is going and living with the intention to make a U-turn and choosing peace.

*In this book, I take a hard look at fear, anxiety, and depression. I define them, discussing the symptoms and causes of each, and how to overcome them. One cannot read this book without being changed from the inside out if the shared truths are taken seriously, acted upon, and allowed to permeate and become a reality in the reader's heart and mind.*

Unfortunately, not knowing how to respond often causes one to react to their depression, anxieties, fears, etc. in ways that promote more of the same. Some are plagued a lot more than others, and some have learned to cope better than others, but there is relief for all of us if we know where to look for it. That is what I hope to accomplish through this short booklet.

It is a quick, easy read and well worth your time. I have learned the antidote to the fear and uncertainty that often leads to anxiety and depression. I want more than anything to share it with you because I am confident you can find relief for your souls through the message I believe the Lord has given me to share with you. Available now on Amazon.

## Living the Life You Always Wanted
### Experience Peace, Joy, Power and Perfect Love in Uncertain Times.

Does the life you are experiencing right now line up with what you know to be what If you were to die today, would most people assume that you were going to heaven as they look at your lifestyle? What you seek is what you get. What are you seeking?

Do you lack peace or joy in your life— feeling stuck in your Christian walk? Do you find yourself wondering if there is more to the "abundant, victorious" life?

Too often, we settle for far less than what God wants to do in and through us. Do you sense that there may be more that God wants to do in and through you than you are currently experiencing?

The cornerstone of the extraordinarily victorious, transformed Christian life is a vital spiritual union with the risen Christ—available only through God's grace. When God created you, He created a masterpiece, and He has an exceptional plan and purpose for your life.

If you are not sure what that is, I hope to help you figure it out with the use of Scripture, referring to our "Life's Manual" (the Bible) as the foundation of that discovery. My second book, *Living the Victorious Life,* will help you to learn how to experience an amazing, abundant, victorious life of peace, joy, power and perfect love.

Do you want to take your life experience to the next level? If our answer is "yes" to any of these questions, then this book is for you.

## OTHER BOOKS BY DEBBY SIBERT COMING SOON:

### *Forever is a Long Time t be Wrong*
#### *What is Your Destiny?*

Do you call yourself an atheist, an agnostic, or a skeptic when it comes to God, Christianity, the reliability of the Bible, the validity of the resurrection, creation and all those Christian buzz words? Maybe you're a "none" – someone who doesn't want to be associated with any religious belief.

Could it be that perhaps you have bought into a lie that all of the above is false? Could it be that you have accepted your parent's beliefs without doing your due diligence to research the truth for yourself?

Could it be that you made a religious decision when you are a child based on what you knew at the time and are stuck there not giving it much thought now that you are older and more mature?

One thing we both can agree on is that someday we will die. I'm telling you that there are only two destinations – heaven and hell, and we don't just return to dust.

If you don't believe that, forever is a long time to be wrong. Once you leave this world, there is no chance to change your mind. It will be too late. The time to get that figured out and straightened out is now while you are still alive.

If you did not want to have anything to do with God while on this earth, He will *not* force you to spend eternity with Him. He will say, *"Thy will be done"* and you will be separated from Him or anything good *forever.*

The purpose of this book is to help walk you through some of the difficult questions with reliable evidence that hopefully will convince you of the need to make a U-turn. We are not promised tomorrow and every breath we take is a gift. Please don't put this off! **Coming February 2021**

## *God's Toolbox for a Fulfilling Marriage*
### *Learn What the Required Tools Are and How to Acquire Them*

This is my fourth book, which is forthcoming, *God's Toolbox for Marriage.* It is still in my head and my heart. I will get it in print as soon as I am able. My husband and I have been mentoring struggling married couples officially for over 15 years, unofficially for decades. This is my passion because I know that an amazing marriage is fully possible and am so sad that many couples never get to experience it, at least after the honeymoon period is over and reality sets in.

Any marriage help book is basically a toolbox of tips regarding how to get along with your spouse in the interest of having a successful marriage. Success looks different to different people, but it goes without saying and would be fair to conclude that we all want to be happy in our relationships.

A "Christian" marriage help book is going to go way beyond the typical psychology of "getting along," In this particular marriage manual, before the various tools for communication, conflict resolution, etc., are discussed, the content is focused on the foundational principles found in Scripture which teaches how to live lives of obedience and surrender to Christ which then gives us the ability to love and serve one another as modeled by Christ.

There is no way we can have the ultimate marriage without having the guidance and direction of the Holy Spirit to empower us to love perfectly with the integrity and humility of Christ. It *IS* possible and this book will give you the tools, encouragement and instruction to achieve an amazing marriage that is the envy of all who know you. **Coming April 2021**

Made in the USA
Middletown, DE
31 October 2020

23098933R00066